THE LITTLE LEAGUE® GUIDE
TO CORRECTING THE 25 MOST
COMMON MISTAKES

D0731219

THE LITTLE LEAGUE® GUIDE
TO CORRECTING THE 25 MOST
COMMON MISTAKES

RECOGNIZING AND REPAIRING
the Mistakes Young Players Make

JOHN MONTELEONE

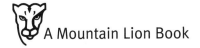 A Mountain Lion Book

Contemporary Books

Chicago   New York   San Francisco   Lisbon   London   Madrid   Mexico City
Milan   New Delhi   San Juan   Seoul   Singapore   Sydney   Toronto

Library of Congress Cataloging-in-Publication Data

Monteleone, John J.
    The Little League guide to correcting the 25 most common mistakes / John
Monteleone.
        p.   cm. — (Little League baseball guides)
    Includes index.
    ISBN 0-07-140887-8
    1. Baseball—Juvenile literature.   2. Little league baseball—Juvenile
literature.   I. Title.   II. Series.

GV867.5.M65   2003
796.357'63—dc21   2002041438

1 2 3 4 5 6 7 8 9 0   AGM/AGM   2 1 0 9 8 7 6 5 4 3

ISBN 0-07-140887-8

Photographs in Chapters 6 through 12 by Beverly Schaefer; all other interior photographs
by the author

This book is dedicated to the memory of George L. Strachan IV of Upper Makefield Township, Pennsylvania, who died of cancer at age 12 on August 20, 1989. George was an accomplished baseball player who played the game he loved every living moment afforded him. Even when he could no longer run the bases he still took his turn at bat.

During his struggle with cancer George became friendly with Larry Bowa, then coach and now manager of the Philadelphia Phillies. He and Bowa often exchanged words of encouragement, with George urging Bowa not to give up when the Phillies played badly. George's indomitable spirit inspired Bowa to remember him: "He thought of me as an idol. I was a hero to him, but really, he was a hero to me."

Contents

Contents

Acknowledgments

This book was conceived and developed by Mountain Lion, Inc., a book producer that specializes in instructional and general reference books in the sports category. A book producer brings together and relies on the special skills of many individuals. The following contributed to developing and producing *The Little League® Guide to Correcting the 25 Most Common Mistakes*, and to all of them we say, "Thank you."

Tom Wilson, researcher and writer, assisted in writing the text and coordinated all the tasks in taking the photographs for the book.

George L. Strachan III arranged for use of the baseball field named after his son, the George L. Strachan IV Field in Upper Makefield Township, Pennsylvania, for taking the photographs in the book.

Bob Johnson and his able-bodied maintenance crew of Upper Makefield Township lent a hand in shaping up the field for our photography session.

Ryan Henritzy, Lee Marvel, Jared Weed, Mike Wilson, Timothy Abbracciamento, Ryan DeAngelis, and Kevin Dragert are the multitalented young baseball players who demonstrated the drills and skills for this book.

Matthew Carnicelli, editor at Contemporary/McGraw-Hill Books, and Craig Bolt, editorial team leader, who shepherded the project for the publisher.

Introduction

I have been around the game of baseball all my life, and have been active on the diamond for more than five decades. I played at every level, from Little League to collegiate to professional baseball, and have coached young players and adults and taught the skills and techniques of hitting, fielding, and pitching to players of all ability levels. Along the way I've learned at least as much as I've taught.

One lesson stands out. Good habits that are learned early pay off every day. That is why I think correcting common mistakes at an early age is not only important but also the single most productive way of improving your overall play. Correcting a player's poor technique at its early stages assures that it does not become ingrained permanently. When you correct a mistake or poor technique in its early stages you sentence it to a very short life. If you let it linger and grow and ultimately become a bad habit it will ruin your performance for as long as you play the game.

I wrote this book to help the thousands of young players who need to learn the correct techniques and skills of baseball in their early years. Every player who takes up this great American pastime does not automatically master the skills that are needed to play it well. Few are what we call "a natural." Yet all players can benefit from comparing their technique or skills against the simple, straightforward instruction that is presented on the following pages. Should you not measure up, then get busy correcting your flaw or fault. Whatever level of accomplishment you bring to this book, there is bound to be a tip or some advice that can improve your play. I guarantee it.

The book is divided into four parts: (1) throwing and receiving mistakes, (2) hitting mistakes, (3) pitching mistakes, and (4) fielding mistakes. Each of the 25 discussions is separate and distinct, although many of the drills and instructional remedies relate to and reinforce others.

You may use this book as your individual skills dictate. It is organized so that you can turn directly to the subject of interest. Each discussion should be read, thought about, tried and practiced, and then reread. By returning to the text and photographs for further reference and study, you will eventually ingrain the motor skills necessary for mastering the aspect of baseball that is of most concern to you.

The Little League® Guide to Correcting the 25 Most Common Mistakes will not only teach you a lot about the proper way to play baseball, it will also help you avoid long periods of time practicing the wrong or incorrect techniques. It will give you the skills to play the game the right way, and it will give them to you early enough in your growth and development to make a difference game by game, day by day, season by season. It will give you a lifetime of pleasure and satisfaction.

THE LITTLE LEAGUE® GUIDE
TO CORRECTING THE 25 MOST
COMMON MISTAKES

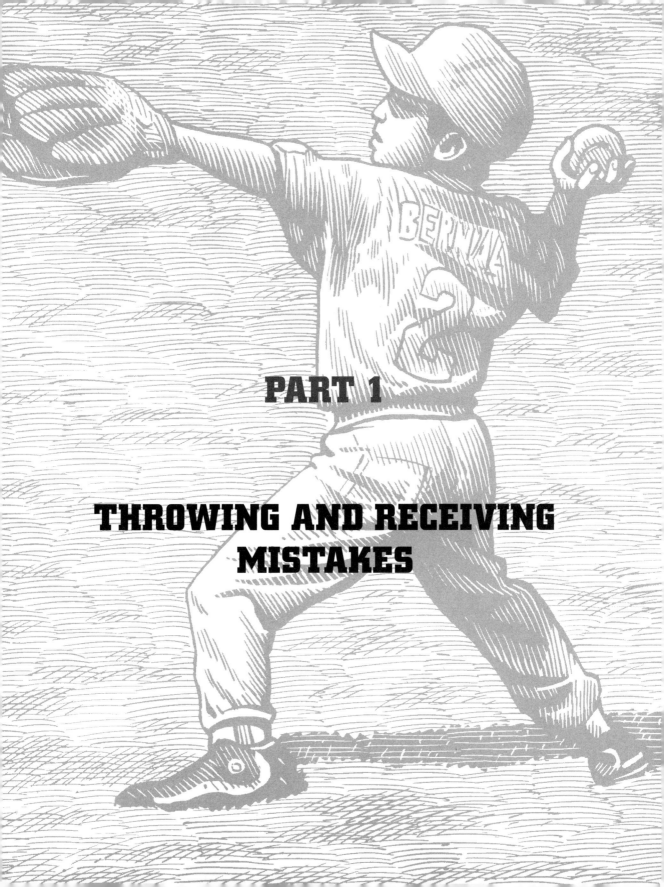

PART 1

THROWING AND RECEIVING MISTAKES

1

FAILING TO SQUARE THE LOWER BODY AND SHOULDERS TO THE TARGET

> Fielding may be comparatively insignificant if the opposing club cannot make any runs off your pitcher. But even the greatest pitching can be hampered by individual fielding faults.
>
> —Branch Rickey

Proper body alignment is a significant part of catching and throwing. The correct position of your body when catching the ball requires that you turn your body slightly to the throwing-hand side. After catching the ball in this position, move naturally and quickly into the throwing motion. This requires you to square the lower and upper body, including the shoulders, when throwing and during the follow-through.

When angling your body to catch a ball on the glove side, step slightly forward with the glove-side leg.

Align your shoulder perpendicular to the target when preparing to throw.

For short throws to the cutoff man, take a crow hop and deliver the ball. Begin a crow hop by stepping toward the target with the stride foot (as shown).

1. Transfer the ball from glove to throwing hand while turning your body completely to the throwing-hand side so that you are sideways (your shoulders are aligned perpendicular) to the target. In other words, align your body so your front shoulder and front foot point to the target.

2. Make a crow hop (two steps on the balls of your feet toward the target) while shifting your weight back and onto your rear leg (throwing-arm side). The

crow hop is initiated by your rear foot and ends on your front foot. Your shoulders remain perpendicular to the target.

3. Swing your throwing arm down and back, fully extended, to create a wide arc. A correct follow-through will then automatically square your lower body and shoulders to the target at the point of release. Note: Keep your eyes focused on the target throughout the process.

It's OK to Be Square

Young players often do not align themselves correctly during the throwing motion. Here are a couple of easy-to-spot violations.

- Throwing across the body: The front foot steps across (for a right-handed player, to the right of) the target line (somewhat like a batter's closed stance), with the glove-hand shoulder closed to the target.
- Opening up your body too much: The front foot steps too far to the glove-hand side of the target. This puts added stress on the shoulder muscles and can lead to injury.

5

Neither of these produces a delivery in which the body is square to the target at the release point and at finish. Here are a few of the problems that may result from failing to square the body properly.

A common throwing mistake occurs when a player plants the stride foot too far to his throwing-hand side (for a right-handed player, too far to his right).

- Inaccurate throws
- Decreased velocity
- Arm strain or injury

Planting the stride foot too far to the glove-hand side is a common mistake in throwing (for a left-handed player, too far to his right).

- Awkward follow-through
- Throws that tail or sink
- Inability to consistently stay on top of the ball (with middle and index fingers on top)

Drill

It is easy to practice the correct method while you are having a simple warm-up catch. But first, without a ball, walk through the correct motion as described earlier. You can also practice this motion in front of a mirror. Then, make throws to your teammate or coach and ask for evaluation.

Sometimes a short, quick sidearm release is the best way to deliver the ball.

The ball can be released from a variety of arm angles. The angle you choose is usually dictated by your body position at the time you catch the ball. Ideally, you want to throw the ball overhand (over the top, or near one o'clock if you imagine the face of a clock) with full arm extension and wide arc. This produces the greatest velocity and distance. However, it is not always possible to throw over the top. Sometimes you need to throw sidearm, three-quarter arm, underhand, or other angles in between.

Your body and mind should instinctively lead you into the correct angle at that time. For example, an infielder charging a slow ground ball is not going to raise up and throw over the top from a bent position. A quick, sidearm throw is more efficient in this situation. Your body position and the speed at which you need to catch and release the ball will naturally lead you to the correct arm angle. That is why it is always important to know the running speed of the batter as well as the runners on base.

Outfielders will most often throw overhand. Infielders, however, must be masters of the multiple arm angles. Watch major-league infielders. Since every ground ball requires them to throw out a runner at one base or another, they are often in a hurry-up mode. They need to catch and throw as quickly as possible. Double plays are a good example. If the second baseman catches the ball belt-high while stepping on second base, he doesn't have the time to fully extend his arm and throw over the top to first base, completing the double play. Instead, he will release it sidearm. It is just quicker.

It seems that infielders have an infinite number of possible body positions at the time they catch the ball—from stretching to reach a ground ball in the hole between shortstop and third base, to charging and bending for a slow roller, to reaching high for a line drive. The resulting arm angles for throws from these positions will all be different. But there is no time to think about it. Instinct should take over.

2

LITTLE OR NO ARMSWING

It don't mean a thing if it ain't got that swing.

—as sung by Ella Fitzgerald

Throwing a baseball requires a certain amount of rhythm and fluidity—much like a golf swing. Golfers swing their arms back, with full extension, to create a wide arc. This gives them greater acceleration and power in their downswing and impact. The same thing applies to throwing a baseball. The greater the arm extension and arc, the greater the arm acceleration and the more velocity on the ball. But some young players seem afraid to use a full armswing, perhaps feeling they can throw more accurately using a short arm throw. This is unfortunate. They need to learn that the only things that affect accuracy and velocity are related to technique, that is, how they execute the throwing motion.

Create an armswing in the shape of a capital letter *C* by starting with your arm down alongside your thigh, then bringing it back and up.

At the top of the *C* the elbow is at shoulder height, and when viewed from the front the release point of the ball is at one o'clock on an imaginary clock face.

The Armswing and Throw

To create a wide armswing, swing your throwing arm down alongside your side and back. Use the momentum from the swing to reach full arm extension and wide arc—similar to a pendulum. You will feel a slight stretching of the shoulder muscles as you reach the end of the backward swing of the arm.

Follow with an overhand (over the top, that is, at one o'clock on an imaginary clock face) throw. Step straight toward the target with the stride foot (non-throwing-side foot), landing on the ball of your foot. Rotate the hips, bring up the throwing arm, elbow of throwing arm at shoulder height. Keep the fingers on top of the ball and the wrist and hand behind it. Bring the arm forward and release the ball alongside the stride foot. Complete the follow-through of the throw by bending slightly at the waist and bringing the arm down toward the knee of the stride foot at a 45-degree angle. Here is a short rhyme, courtesy of baseball coach Mickey Kessler, that

11

Step directly toward the target when throwing the ball.

Fingers are behind and on top of the ball, and the elbow of the throwing arm is at shoulder height.

will help you make a proper throw: "Thumb to the *thigh*, elbow *high*, fingers to the *sky*, wave *bye-bye*!"

Let the throw fit the situation. If you have a long throw from the outfield, a wide armswing is certainly preferred. However, if you are charging a ground ball and need to make a quick throw to a base while bending low to the ground, then a short arm throw (maybe a sidearm) is most efficient. Infielders often use the sidearm throw. It's just a short, quick, snap throw with a bent elbow and a lot of wrist action. You be the judge. But, whenever possible, rely on a wide armswing and throw over the top.

Watch major-league outfielders who have strong arms and use proper technique. Vladimir Guerrero is an example. His rifle arm and accuracy can be attributed not only to his natural physical gifts but also to excellent form and execution. Not all players are blessed with the same degree of natural skills, but all possess the same opportunity to learn the correct methods. This then makes it possible for everyone to reach their highest potential.

Smooth and Easy

Have you ever watched the smooth, powerful swings of top professional golfers like Tiger Woods and Ernie Els, or the seemingly effortless golf swing of the legendary Sam Snead? It looks like they are hardly swinging the club, yet they hit the ball so far. Well, part of it has to do with the wide arc created by the full extension of their arms. And they do it with such a rhythmic and graceful motion. Actually, smooth and easy is also very important in achieving a long, flowing armswing when you throw a baseball. If you are nervous or tight, the tension in your muscles restricts your armswing. As a result, you lock your wrists and "short-arm" the ball. This makes it look like the ball is coming out of the thrower's ear, similar to a shot-put toss. Baseball, as with most sports, should be played tension free—kind of loosey-goosey. Doubt and fear are the usual suspects when your body decides to freeze up. Maybe you become afraid of making an inaccurate throw in an important game situation. That is when it is especially important to loosen up so you can obtain a fluid arm motion that produces maximum velocity on the throw.

13

Drill

Here is an easy drill that you can do in front of a large mirror, without a ball or glove. Stand sideways to the mirror and look at it out of the corner of your eye as you perform this drill. Hold your two hands against your chest. Shift your weight back and swing your throwing hand back with force to its full extension. Then step forward with your glove-side foot and bring your throwing hand over the top. Complete the motion with a weight shift to the front, then the follow-through. Repeat as often as necessary to make it an automatic movement.

A common throwing mistake is to "short-arm" the ball—that is, move the arm and hand forward without extension and too close to the side of the head.

Catch the ball with two hands whenever you don't have to reach far away from the body to get to it.

When catching with two hands, align the bare hand alongside the glove's thumb on balls caught above the waist (left). After the ball enters the glove use the bare hand to cover the opening of the glove (right) or slip it slightly inside to hold the ball inside the pocket.

The techniques used in playing the game of baseball have been refined greatly since baseball began in the nineteenth century. Early players had to experiment through trial and error to determine the most efficient and productive ways to field, throw, hit, run the bases, and so on. Their equipment was primitive by today's standards, yet benefits were derived from this. For example, their tiny gloves made it imperative to catch the ball with two hands in order to keep the ball from falling out and to remove the ball quickly. Although today's gloves are much larger and better designed, players are still advised to catch with two hands for the same reasons as in those early years.

Baseball's evolution has reached the point where today's advanced methods and techniques are available to everyone, whether through books, videos, training camps, or just watching professional players. Use them to your advantage and enjoyment.

3

ABBREVIATED FOLLOW-THROUGH

> The adage "Practice makes perfect" is not true unless the practice sessions are instructive, done with enthusiasm, and done correctly.
>
> —Danny Litwiler, major-league player and collegiate baseball Hall of Fame coach

An adage that parents often pass on to their children says "Finish what you start." Usually used in reference to a project or task, it means never leave a job undone or never give up on a job. The same thing can be said for throwing a baseball. Since the maximum velocity on a thrown ball is derived from a complete follow-through, always finish what you start. That is, make a full follow-through. It is similar to hitting a baseball or golf ball. The ball will not travel as far if you quit on the swing after contact is made. Likewise, a baseball thrown without a follow-through will not travel as fast or as far.

In the follow-through, bring the throwing arm down and alongside the outside of the stride leg in a sweeping 45-degree arc.

18

What Does It Mean?

When a follow-through is executed correctly, the forward momentum of your body allows your throwing arm to naturally flow down and finish on the outside of your opposite leg. Done properly, the throwing hand follows the glove hand at a 45-degree angle.

This "follow-the-leader" move produces full extension and maximizes the velocity on the ball. The rest of your body must follow through, too. In fact, it is impossible to obtain full arm extension without getting your entire body into the process. Young players sometimes stop their arms abruptly after releasing the ball. Picture a dart player's short stroke, which is more like a jab. This motion, when used in throwing a baseball, creates tension, reduces velocity, and affects accuracy. It can also result in a sore arm or injury.

Do not stop the arm upon release of the ball.

Let Loose

Regardless of whether you throw overhand, three-quarter arm, or sidearm, a follow-through is necessary. With an overhand or three-quarter throw, push off your rear foot and step forward onto the front foot (like a pitcher stepping toward the plate to make a pitch delivery). Bring your throwing arm forward, elbow at shoulder height, fingers on top of the ball, and wrist and hand behind it. Release the ball just before or alongside your planted stride foot as your hand travels forward.

Release the ball over the stride foot and keep the arm moving down and across the thigh of the stride leg.

The rest of your body also goes forward. Let your rear leg swing forward (past neutral) after you transfer your weight to your glove-side leg. Extend your throwing arm fully down and outside of your opposite leg (picture the hand traveling in a 45-degree arc). Have your glove hand finish alongside you and avoid swinging it too far to the rear of your body.

19

Your body should end up in a slightly lower position, bent at the waist, with knees flexed and eyes looking forward. A practice that helps to ingrain bending at the waist and rotation of the hips is to exaggerate the follow-through to the point where your throwing hand touches the ground at the end. *Caution:* This is not the desired form, only a drill that will help promote a good follow-through and avoid "short-arming" the throw.

Keep the glove alongside the body, not in the back, when releasing the ball and following through.

Practice your follow-through by picking up grass or a ball resting just outside your stride foot.

Let the arm follow its natural course without consciously stopping it or altering its direction. It should flow naturally to its destination by itself. This tension-free release produces a smooth, strong, and accurate throw. Keep your head up with eyes on the target throughout, while maintaining complete body control.

Young players sometimes decelerate after releasing the ball—almost as if the release point represents the end of the throwing motion. Perhaps they are tentative and afraid that a full motion will create an inaccurate throw, whereas the opposite is true. Does a professional tennis player stop her racket after hitting her serve? No, she lets the racket and arm momentum carry through. Watch a professional quarterback throw a 50-yard pass. You can be sure that he lets his body and arm follow through—unless, of course, a 300-pound defensive tackle interrupts his follow-through.

Golf legend Gary Player placed high value on the follow-through. In fact, it was not uncommon for his momentum to carry him a step or two toward the target after the follow-through. That is unusual for a golfer, but it emphasizes the importance of getting your full body into the process for maximum power and velocity. Similarly, some major-league outfielders' momentum carries them a few steps forward after they release the ball and follow through.

Drill

The best way to correct an abbreviated follow-through is simply by practice, which not only reinforces the correct form but builds arm strength. First, simulate the throwing motion in front of a mirror without a ball. Repeat the motion and look for these keys: (1) your

Raise the throwing-arm elbow to the height of the shoulder.

throwing arm approaches the release point with the elbow at shoulder height; (2) your throwing arm fully extends as it crosses over your body and finishes outside your opposite leg; (3) your knees are slightly flexed and your upper body is bending at the waist; (4) your head is up and looking ahead and you finish with your hips square to the target. Next, go to the field and make long throws from the outfield to home plate. Or throw a tennis ball against a wall, aiming at a spot or square on the wall. Let your coach evaluate your form.

22

The purpose of the full follow-through, of course, is to produce maximum velocity, distance, and accuracy. Part of the accuracy, however, depends on the type of grip you have on the ball. Ideally, you want the ball to travel on a straight line to your destination—not tail away, sink, or rise. This is done by gripping the ball with your middle and index fingers across the horseshoe seams. This is also known as the four-seam grip. Use this grip for every throw you make. It will go straighter, farther, and stay in the air longer. All position players should use this grip. It takes practice, however, to find this grip each time you remove the ball from your glove. But it must become something you do automatically. Otherwise, despite your good form and follow-through, some of your throws could run off course. Also, hold the ball loosely rather than choking it with a tight grip. Don't place it too close to the palm of your hand; hold it in your fingers. Keep space between your fingers and palm. Place your thumb under the ball.

4

FAILING TO CRADLE THE BALL WHEN CATCHING IT

Find a glove that fits comfortably, one that you can control. The idea [when catching a ball] is to close the fingers of the glove around the ball so the ball will not drop out.

—Jeff Burroughs, major-league player and
Little League world championship coach

Phrases like "soft hands" and "cradling the ball" are heard frequently when coaches describe talented fielders. But what do they really mean? Both descriptions refer to the gentle way of letting the ball enter the glove and letting the hands "give," that is, bringing the glove back toward the body as the ball enters the glove. This reduces the impact (and the accompanying sting) and gives you a better feel for the ball—the next best thing to holding the ball in your bare hands. Although the ball is not touching your hand directly, cradling provides this sense of where the ball is in your glove so you can remove it confidently and quickly.

It's a common mistake to catch an overhead ball with a stiff arm.

Think of catching the ball bare-handed. Hopefully, you would not leave your hands stiff in the extended position, letting the full force of the ball hit your bare hand. Instead, you would bring your hands back toward your body—or give—as the ball arrives in your hands. This reduces the sting and lets you sense the location of the ball in your glove.

24

Symptoms

Poor mechanics result in "hard hands," thus making it difficult to catch the ball in the correct area of the glove and increasing the chance that you will drop the ball. Young players have a tendency to hold their gloves at full arms' length, straight out, aiming the glove at the ball—letting ball hit glove. The glove acts and looks more like a shield than a receiving device. This "ball meets wall" technique creates hard hands, making cradling impossible. Also, some players stab at the ball. As the ball arrives, they thrust the glove straight out to meet the ball (the direct opposite of what should be done). This creates even greater force at impact. Not only is it more likely that you'll drop the ball, but your hands will probably sting for quite some time.

How to Cradle

Catch the ball in the palm of the glove, not the webbing, especially when you need to retrieve the ball quickly. This gives you a good

Stabbing at the ball to catch it is a common mistake.

feel for the ball, a sense of where it is so you can find it and remove it quickly. It simulates the efficiency of the small mitts used in the early eras of baseball. Films of early baseball players serve as excellent models of cradling. Their gloves were not much bigger than their hands, so they literally caught the ball in their hands. If you catch the ball in the webbing, you can lose sense of its location. The ball can even get stuck in the web, making it difficult to get it out on your first attempt.

If you want your hands to give and cradle the ball, your hands must be relaxed and free from tension as the ball arrives. Extend your arms slightly toward the ball, then bring them back to your body along with the ball, allowing your hands to give and cradle. This smooth movement then flows naturally into the throwing motion.

Catching the ball with bare hands will prepare you to correctly use your hands when receiving the ball in the pocket of your glove.

Drill

This bare-hand drill is simple but effective. Two players toss a ball to each other, aiming chest-high. The receiver extends both hands toward the ball and catches the ball while bringing both hands back toward the body. If done correctly, the receiver should sense the cradling effect and the deadening of the force from the ball. Substitute raw eggs for baseballs and repeat. And watch the fun (and increased concentration!).

26

A wide variety of gloves are on the market now. They are much bigger than years ago, so be careful when selecting your glove. Big is not necessarily best, particularly for young players. It isn't unusual to see youngsters with gloves that seem almost as big as they are. Since many youngsters gravitate to large gloves, a knowledgeable person should help make the selection. Children are probably influenced by what they see professional players wearing. They may also think that it is easier to catch a ball with a big glove. But that is not always true. Big gloves can be very heavy and unwieldy on a young person's hand.

A small glove is the best choice for a young player because it is easy to control and helps the player learn the proper way to catch and release the ball. Major-league outfielders use large gloves, but that isn't something to be copied by young players who have small hands and are still learning the proper catching techniques. Notice,

Younger players should use smaller gloves that can be more easily manipulated.

however, that middle infielders (shortstop and second basemen) use much smaller gloves than outfielders. This is due to their need to find and remove the ball from their gloves quickly in many situations, such as the double play. Hall of Fame second basemen Joe Morgan (Cincinnati Reds) and Bill Mazeroski (Pittsburgh Pirates) used smaller gloves (gloves with 13-inch fingers as opposed to the 17-inch gloves that pitchers and outfielders used) for this reason. They were two of the very best at turning the double play, and their glove selection was a major factor in their success.

Actually, young players can't go wrong by using a small glove, regardless of what position they play. As they grow physically and increase their skills, they can also grow into larger gloves if the position warrants. At a young age, however, the emphasis should be on receiving the ball softly in the area of the glove where you have the best feel for the ball. That is accomplished most easily with a smaller glove.

5

CATCHING THE BALL OFF TO THE SIDE OF THE BODY

> *Outfielders who take the double step after catching a fly ball seldom throw out anybody, although they may have marvelous arms with correct trajectory.*
>
> —Branch Rickey

Imagine this picture for a moment. A player is about to catch a fly ball, positioned under the ball, waiting for it to come down. The player's body is turned slightly toward the throwing hand. But then, instead of catching the ball on the throwing-hand side, the player catches it on the opposite side of the body, resembling the Statue of Liberty. The player's glove hand reaches up and away from the body—like Lady Liberty's torch. As a result, the body opens up toward the glove side. The player must take extra steps to get in position for the throw to the infield.

The correct method, of course, is to catch the fly ball on the throwing-hand side, and the direction your body should be angled.

Several problems can result from catching the ball off to the side:

- It is more difficult to adjust to a ball that drifts off course at the last moment.
- It is harder to catch the ball with two hands.
- It takes longer to get the ball back across your body and into the throwing motion.
- The ball is not squarely in your line of sight.
- You may become unbalanced and need to shift weight over to the throwing side.

Make It Easy on Yourself

30

The proper and most efficient place to catch the ball is over the throwing shoulder. This leads directly down and into the throwing motion. Catching the ball off to the side of the body delays the release of the ball, which can be detrimental when attempting to throw a runner out. Such little things may seem insignificant, but they consume precious time, giving the runner an extra step or two. Naturally, this refers to a situation where the fielder gets to the ball in sufficient time to square the body to the ball. In such a case, there is no reason to catch it to the side of the body.

Think about it. Why go through the effort of getting to the ball in time, and then catch it at the side? It gets back to funda-

Whenever an outfielder needs to make a prompt throw after catching a fly ball, he should catch the ball over the throwing-side shoulder. It reduces the time needed to throw the ball back to the infield.

mentals. Baseball is a game of calculations—making the most efficient use of movement, space, and time. And it all adds up to gaining the greatest advantage in a particular situation. Each play should be analyzed in this way. The mind plays a major role, not only in the planning, but also in the discipline required to carry out the plan.

Drill

Correcting this flaw should be easy. It is purely mind over matter. Understand the correct method and practice it. Ask a coach or teammate to throw easy fly balls directly at you. Position your body as explained in Mistake 25, "Catching the Ball Above the Head." Then catch the ball over your throwing-hand shoulder—not on the opposite side of your body. Repeat the drill.

Some people may consider catching the ball on the side of the body a cool play. But think of what you are trying to accomplish. The play does not always end with the catch. It can involve throwing a runner out or preventing a run from scoring. Is the cool and casual look more beneficial to you and your team than the practical and efficient method? That goes for other plays as well. You see players on TV making "highlight-film catches." Some are authentic, meaning they are necessary to making the play. However, others are designed to look more difficult than they really are, thus attracting attention to the player. The diving catch is an example. Diving should be your last resort. Whenever possible, catch the ball while remaining on your feet. By diving you remove yourself temporarily from the play until you can get back on your feet and regain your balance to make a throw.

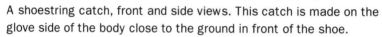

A shoestring catch, front and side views. This catch is made on the glove side of the body close to the ground in front of the shoe.

The shoestring catch is rarely seen or mentioned anymore, but it is a model of efficiency, beauty, and athleticism. The play is made by running in toward a fly ball or line drive, then bending over and catching the ball at your feet—just before the ball hits the ground. It is a great play that shows the fielder's ability to make a difficult catch look easy. It also enables him to finish the rest of the play without interruption because he remains on his feet. A good policy is to try to make every catch and play look easy, not difficult or cool. Save that for the backyard.

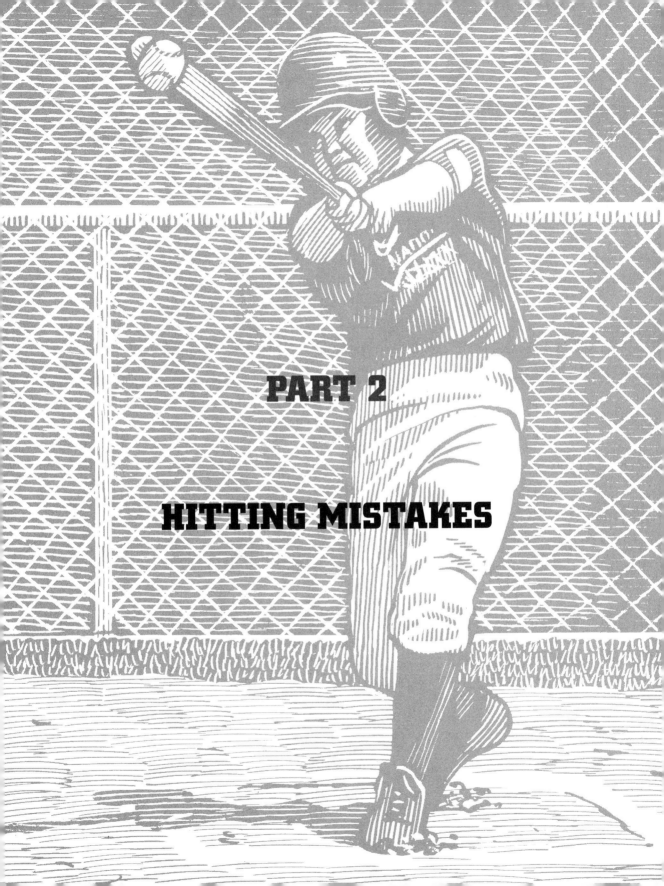

PART 2

HITTING MISTAKES

6

POOR BALANCE
IN THE STANCE

Balance is a crucial factor in any sport. Golf, tennis, football, basketball—take your pick. You'll never see a successful performer in any of these activities who isn't on balance most of the time. The same thing is true for baseball. Small wonder that balance is one of the chief goals of a batter's stance.

—Charley Lau

There are no fixed guidelines for the batting stance. Stances vary greatly, but most batters take up a position with their feet approximately shoulder-width apart, or slightly wider, with some flex in their knees and their arms and hands held slightly in front of the body. But how you stand in the batter's box is dictated by what feels comfortable and, ultimately, what is workable.

Some players, such as Edgar Martinez and Julio Franco, hold the bat high, pointing the head of the barrel toward the sky or even the pitcher. Others, such as Todd Zeile, hold the bat up and down in

Players set up in the batter's box in many different stances. Julio Franco's stance looks like this.

Todd Zeile puts the bat in front of his chest and holds it almost vertical.

The stances of Franco and Zeile work because each brings his hands and bat to the launch position before attacking the pitch.

front of their chest as they await the pitch. A batter's stance is a matter of personal comfort, and it really doesn't matter how you stand as long as the stance allows a simple, short movement of the bat to the launch position (the position just in front of the rear shoulder from which the swing is started or launched).

If you're holding your hands or setting up your feet in a manner that makes it difficult to get into that position, you need to make an adjustment. The best approach is to start with a basic batting stance and work from there. If you need to make a minor adjustment or add a subtle movement, make the change from a basic position.

A basic or standard batting stance brings comfort and balance. First, place your feet just outside your shoulders and hips. To align yourself properly place a bat in a vertical position just inside each

The "athletic stance" includes feet spread slightly more than shoulder-width apart, legs and back slightly bent, and shoulders level. The front shoulder should tilt slightly downward with a bat in hand so that the player can more easily bring the bat down into the strike zone.

instep. The bat should intersect with the hip on each side—this places your hips just inside the feet, a position that allows you to rotate easily.

Assume the "athletic position," that is, flex your knees slightly and bend at the waist. Keep your upper body tall, with your shoulders aligned parallel to an imaginary line from the center of the pitcher's rubber to the center of home plate. Hold your hands at about shoulder level, aligned with the inside of your rear shoulder, approximately four to six inches in front of your body.

The athletic position puts most of your weight on the balls of the feet. You can stabilize and control your upper-body weight, moving it from backward to forward, or rotating it around an axis (your spine). No one can move efficiently in any sport from anything other than this position of balance and flexibility.

Test for Good Balance

Here is a quick test to see if you have established a balanced, workable stance. Ask a parent, coach, or teammate to place his fingers on your sternum and push as if he were opening a swinging door for a few inches. Then have him place his hand in the middle of your back and push again. If you cannot stay stable, that is, if you cannot maintain your stance without falling forward or backward, then you need to adjust your stance. It is not balanced and you will have trouble hitting from the position you've adopted.

Signs of Bad Balance

Almost any Little League game offers an opportunity to see the results of improper balance in the batting stance. Here are a few mistakes that you might recognize, and if you do, make an effort to make an adjustment.

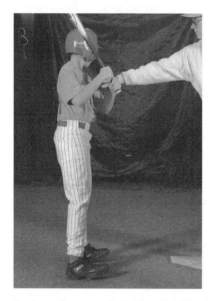

A player in a comfortable athletic stance will not lose his balance or stability when pushed gently on the sternum or the middle of the back (top). But a player with improper stance, such as feet not placed at least shoulder-width apart, will lose his balance and stability (bottom).

- Standing flat-footed
- Standing straight-legged, or with no flex at the knees
- Feet too close together
- Falling away from the plate when finishing the swing
- "Hot feet," that is, feet are moving (usually back, then forward) while pitch is in flight toward the plate
- Weight of batter shifts to the heels when reacting to the pitch

Standing stiff- or straight-legged is a typical batting stance flaw.

Standing with the feet too close together is another common mistake.

Standing with the weight on the heels is yet another common mistake.

Drill

Players who shift their weight improperly to their heels lose the athleticism—balance and agility—that are necessary for moving into and attacking the pitch. Here is a drill that you can practice outside or in front of a mirror to keep your weight over the body's axis (spine) and thus your balance throughout the swing. Place a broomstick or other long stick in the ground alongside your front or leading hip (left hip for a right-handed batter). It should be one to two inches to the side of your hip, just enough for you to rotate without disturbing it. Take your normal stance beside the broomstick, and then take your stride and swing. Check to see that your rotation does not touch the broomstick, and make sure that you do not fall into it as you finish the swing. Repeat 25 times.

To check your balance and control during the stride and swing, stand with a broomstick or a batting tee about three to four inches from your leading hip. Swing, rotating the hips. If your hip swings freely and does not touch the stick or tee, your balance is OK and your stride is in the right direction (toward the pitcher).

7

STEPPING IN THE BUCKET

> *Kids should stride directly toward the pitchers. A lot of young kids either have a little fear of the baseball or are trying to pull everything. Take a short stride back or at the pitcher for the best results.*
>
> —Mark McGwire

Striding open—or what is commonly called stepping in the bucket—takes the hitter's lead foot away from home plate. It is one of the most common mistakes young players make.

Fear of being struck by the ball is the primary cause of stepping in the bucket. It is natural to recoil when anything is thrown toward you, but you can learn how to control this natural reaction. To overcome this, young players must learn how to avoid being hit by a pitch and to practice attacking pitches that approach them over the plate.

Striding away from the pitcher toward foul territory is a common hitting mistake called stepping in the bucket.

Drill

Here is a simple drill that can help. Mark off an area 17 inches wide to serve as a makeshift home plate. Have a coach or buddy set up 10 to 12 feet in front of you with a dozen rolled-up socks and softly toss the socks to you in an underhand motion. Swing at any pitch that crosses the plate between the shoulders and knees and take those pitches that miss the strike zone.

Then have your helper toss the socks in an overhand motion on bended knee. This will accelerate the speed of the pitches and acclimate you to the overhand throwing motion.

This drill is also a good time to practice protecting yourself from pitches that miss the strike zone and hit you. The photo opposite shows how to roll the lead shoulder down and away from inside pitches. In other words, when a pitch comes inside and close to you,

The safest way to avoid injury from being struck by a pitch is to roll up the lead shoulder and roll the head down and away. And remember to wear a helmet.

you should immediately turn away, closing the front side and thus exposing your side or back to the ball. To get an understanding of this movement, practice spinning clockwise (for right-handed hitter) as quickly as possible. In the spin, you should also lower your head while simultaneously raising your front shoulder to protect the side of your face.

Happy Feet

Young players often step in the bucket as a result of what is called "happy feet." This is when the player continues to move the feet throughout the at bat. As the pitch is released, he finds himself still moving his feet around in the batter's box. The pitch is on the way

Stride toward the pitcher.

and the batter is not ready; his feet are not positioned to react. A batter will often step back with the rear foot and then toward foul ground—away from home plate—with the lead foot. Happy feet are the surest way to a sad at bat. Without a settled stance and firm rear foot to push off from, the player has little hope of making contact and no chance of getting on base.

Drill

Set yourself up in a square stance (feet parallel to an imaginary line from home plate to the pitcher's mound). Place two bats on the ground perpendicular to your lead foot. One bat should extend out from just off your toe toward the pitcher's mound, and the other from just off your heel to the pitcher's mound. Take your stride and make sure your foot remains between the two bats. If you set up initially with an open or closed stance, keep the bats in the same position but remember to finish your stride with the feet in the square position.

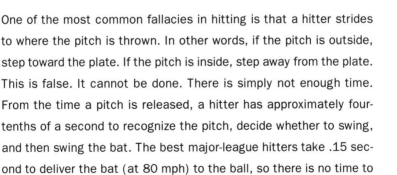

One of the most common fallacies in hitting is that a hitter strides to where the pitch is thrown. In other words, if the pitch is outside, step toward the plate. If the pitch is inside, step away from the plate. This is false. It cannot be done. There is simply not enough time. From the time a pitch is released, a hitter has approximately four-tenths of a second to recognize the pitch, decide whether to swing, and then swing the bat. The best major-league hitters take .15 second to deliver the bat (at 80 mph) to the ball, so there is no time to step *to* swing. It's always step *and* swing, and the step is always just before or just as the ball is released from the pitcher's hand.

8

FEAR OF BEING STRUCK BY THE BALL

You can't be afraid of the baseball. You've got to attack the baseball.

—Jay Bell

Fear of being struck by a pitched ball and stepping in the bucket are closely linked. Usually, the latter follows closely on the heels of the former. Unfortunately, fear of being hit by the ball produces more than one batting fault.

Fear diminishes a batter's confidence. It misdirects your focus from attacking the ball to avoiding it. Fear disrupts a batter's timing. When you add the time it takes to determine if the ball is coming directly at your body, you cannot react in time to meet the ball as it crosses the plate. Fear distracts and immobilizes. If not overcome, it will turn every at bat into an exercise in futility. As former Boston Red Sox player and Hall of Famer Carl Yastrzemski remarked, "If you're afraid of being hit, you might as well not bother going up to the plate at all. You can't hit the ball if you're afraid it will hit you."

Stepping in the bucket—that is, stepping away from the plate when a pitch is thrown—is still the most common result of fear. Pitchers, including those at the Little League level who are skilled enough, will take advantage by throwing pitches that move either from the inside of the plate to the middle or from the middle to the outside of the plate. Batters who are stepping in the bucket and thus pulling their bodies away from the plate—that is, the hitting zone— cannot reach these pitches.

Fear will reduce you to a one-dimensional hitter—the only pitch you'll have any chance of contacting is an inside fastball. Even curveballs that break over the inside of the plate won't be hittable because a fearful batter will flinch when the pitch starts toward the body before breaking over the plate.

52

When you're afraid of being struck by the ball the result is a stride away from the pitcher.

Fear can be overcome. Players need to replace their fears with a healthy respect for what can happen if they are struck by a pitch. They need to learn how to deal with errant or brushback pitches, and they need to focus on the knowledge that getting hit by a pitched ball is not a frequent occurrence and that it rarely results in serious injury.

How to Avoid Injury

One way to diminish the fear of getting hit is to learn how to defend yourself when batting. To avoid serious injury when a ball is bearing down on you, simply tuck your head behind your front shoulder and roll your lead shoulder down and away from the pitch. You should immediately turn away, closing the front side and thus exposing your side or back to the ball. Your helmet will pro-

Striding away from the pitcher causes poor plate coverage. The pitches over the outside corner cannot be reached with the bat.

tect you from serious injury if the ball strikes you in the head or ear area.

If you continue moving toward the pitcher or spin toward foul territory—thus opening the front of your body to being struck by the pitch—you risk serious injury, such as a bruised or broken hand or wrist bone. Some batters fly open more than others when a pitch comes too far inside. For these batters, wearing protection that covers the lower and upper arm closest to the pitcher is the only way to guarantee protection from injury.

Drill

Balls thrown toward you that are above the waist present the greatest chance for injury. Here is a drill that will help protect you from getting seriously hurt.

You will need a dozen pairs of rolled-up socks and a dozen tennis balls. Have a buddy or coach pitch the socks, mixing strikes with balls and pitches that hit you. Practice rolling away from the pitches, tucking your head and pulling your arms, wrists, and hands into and behind the body, in effect, placing your back between you and the oncoming ball. You may drop the bat. When you absolutely cannot avoid being struck, allow the ball to hit you in the side or on the back. Do this drill with 25 to 30 pitches and then switch to the tennis balls and repeat. When you feel confident that you've mastered the technique, repeat with baseballs at soft-toss speed.

Once you are convinced that you can survive an errant pitch you will have put two very important weapons in your hitting arsenal—confidence and a ball-attacking frame of mind. You are on your way to becoming a great hitter. Ty Cobb summed this up nicely: "Every great hitter works on the theory that the pitcher is more afraid of him than he is of the pitcher."

9

DROPPING THE REAR SHOULDER, OR UPPERCUTTING

> *Line drives come from swinging down to the ball and through it, not up at it.*
>
> —Doug Glanville

Many young players use a bat that is too heavy, especially one that has too much weight in the barrel. When a bat is too heavy, the hands cannot control the barrel. As a result, the weight of the barrel drops the hands below the hitting plane in the downswing. When players try to adjust—that is, get the bat on plane—they move upward, passing through the plane on which the pitch is traveling. The swing is not only an uppercut, but also a late uppercut. The bat passes into the plane of the incoming pitch after the ball has sped past the bat into the catcher's mitt.

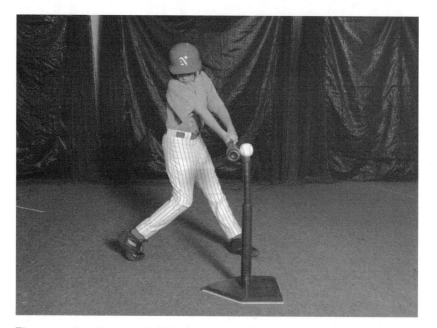

The correct path to the ball is down from the launch position (top) and then level and slightly up (bottom) as the swing leaves the hitting zone.

Thus many young players suffer from the fault of uppercutting, which is when you create a low-to-high path to the pitch that is angled too severely. Any action that creates a severely angled path from low to high, or high to low, is flawed. An uppercut swing is too severely angled when the bat starts below the projected path of the pitch, travels through the hitting plane for a very short space, and then quickly moves above the plane.

Tee Ball can promote uppercutting because batters realize that their best chance at hitting a stationary ball for distance (and carry) is to drop the hands and uppercut, thus creating a fly-ball arc. So watch out—you may become an all-star hitter in Tee Ball and an all-American out in baseball.

Another cause of uppercutting is hitching, that is, dropping the hands while in the stance below the launch position (which is just

The incorrect path to the ball is from low to high.

above and behind the rear shoulder) and starting the swing from this lowered position. Hitches are not always detrimental. They can provide a powerful trigger or loading action, and they can keep a player tension-free by providing important pre-swing motion.

But a player must complete the hitching in time to react to the oncoming pitch. Many successful hitters, such as Darryl Strawberry, have successfully used a hitch in their swings and are able to bring their hands back up to the launch position in time to attack the pitch. As a rule, however, it is not advisable to build a hitch—especially one that drops the hands several inches—into a swing. It is better to ride the hands back slightly, perhaps two to three inches, and then bring them forward from the launch position into the hitting area.

Hitching, when the hands drop down below the waist to start the approach to the ball, is another cause of uppercutting.

A long down-and-up hitch causes you to swing too severely from low to high and makes it nearly impossible to get the barrel squared at impact. One solution for young players who have a slightly heavy bat is to choke up. This brings the bat under control and should result in better manipulation of the barrel throughout the swing. In other words, you should swing more level, or on plane longer.

Choking up is a good way to fully control the bat for a young player who hasn't yet developed strong hands, wrists, and arms.

The correct swing travels from the launch position (bat held shoulder-high or slightly above the shoulder, hands and wrists in cocked position) into the downswing along a shallow angle to a point that is directly in the path of the ball. Unlike golf where the ball rests in the same spot time after time, this point is not in one consistent location. It is a spot in the strike zone along the bat's path at which the ball and bat collide or intersect. Its location is within the strike zone, that is, over the plate and between the bottom of the knee and just above the belt.

Once the bat is moving along the same plane that the pitch is traveling, it needs to continue along that path through contact. To roll the top hand over immediately after contact would require perfect timing on all pitches, which is virtually impossible. Strive to make contact with the palm of the top hand facing skyward. Roll it over—that is, rotate the wrists counterclockwise after contact.

At impact the top hand is palm up on the bat and the bottom hand is palm down on the bat.

Drill

Using a batting tee, place the ball in the center of the plate at the following heights: (1) letter-high, (2) midway between the letters and belt, and (3) belt-high. At each position, hit 10 line drives straight through the pitcher's box, balls that would carry into center field for line-drive singles.

Choke up on the bat. On the downswing move the knob of the bat to the level of the pitch just as your hands move past your rear hip and continue forward of your midsection. Keep your hands in the palm-down (bottom hand), palm-up (top hand) position as long as possible, at least until you strike the ball. Continue this drill until you can hit 10 consecutive line drives at each position.

Players who are nine years old or younger should have a coach or friend pitch to them from a kneeling position so that the pitch trajectory will not be too steep. This will prevent batters from creating a low-to-high swing plane in an effort to get the bat on plane and meet the ball squarely.

Kneel down when pitching to young players. This will lower the arc of the pitches.

10

LUNGING OR REACHING FOR THE BALL

Let it travel, let it travel.

—Gary "Sarge" Matthews, Sr.

I'm six-foot-three and have a lot of leverage, so I'm able to get out on my front foot but maintain control of my weight shift. Often hitters who try to do this get too far out on their front foot and shift their weight forward incorrectly. This will result in a lot of ground balls.

—Alex Rodriguez

When Gary "Sarge" Matthews, Sr., a major-league all-star outfielder of the 1970s and 1980s, and Alex Rodriguez, arguably the greatest all-around shortstop in major-league history, made their respective comments they were addressing the same problem—lunging or reaching for the ball.

Lunging or reaching for the ball occurs when you allow your weight to move too far forward. When it moves too far it can also roll away from the center or axis of your body, that is, toward foul territory. So this makes full plate coverage nearly impossible.

Lunging also produces another problem—it speeds up the pitches. When you lunge, your head moves rapidly for a foot or so, making the pitches harder to track and catch up to.

When you lunge or reach for the ball you have no chance of putting a charge into a pitch. Instead, you will produce weak grounders and fly balls—nothing but easy outs! You'll know you're lunging when you lose balance and fall forward or sideways, when you can't reach pitches that are on the outside part of the plate, and when pitches seem to get to you before you can react.

Causes of the Problem

This flaw can be traced to poor balance in the swing and poor technique in the stride. Many players first get in trouble with an overly aggressive movement toward the pitcher. They bring the entire backside forward, from top to bottom. Yes, you need to step toward the pitcher, but at the same time you must make a quiet, short step that does not thrust the weight of the body over or beyond the front leg.

Step toward the pitcher but keep the weight behind the point of contact with the ball and keep the hands back, cocked and ready to bring the bat forward in a flash. Keep the weight either centered over the hips or slightly on the back leg until you're ready to unload the weight to the front leg and rotate the hips. When you commit to swing, simply allow the hips to rotate (around and against the front leg, which acts like a hub). You'll feel the arms and hands gaining speed along the arc of the swing. If you lunge or reach for the ball, it is impossible to reach this position. Improper control

In the setup the hands are held slightly in front of the rear shoulder and chest (top). In the stride the hands go to the launch position directly above and partially behind the rear shoulder. Do not wrap the hands or bat around the back of the head or shoulders (bottom).

and transfer of your weight ruins your balance and brings on the dreaded lunge.

Poor technique in the stride includes the failure to brace the front leg properly. As the weight moves forward from the backside to the front side during the swing, the front leg braces, that is, it becomes a post around and into which the torso and hips rotate. If this leg does not stiffen and contain the weight shift, the momentum of the weight shift brings the weight forward and to the outside of the plant foot. Again, the results are a loss of balance and a powerless swing.

Another stride-related cause of lunging or reaching for the ball is the continual forward movement of the top half of the body. This forces the leg to flex in an effort to control the weight that is passing forward of the knee and plant foot. When it flexes, your hip rotation is reduced (and so is your power).

The stride leg forms a post that is straight or slightly bent at the knee. The hips rotate while the stride leg remains firmly planted in place. The head stays behind the point of impact.

A common mistake is to move the top half of the body too far forward over the front leg. This reduces power and bat speed.

Another cause is failing to uncoil into the front leg. This flaw begins with the stance of the early part of the swing when the batter fails to close or square the hips. Without a coiling or closing of the hips, the only way to build momentum is to make a vigorous shift toward the pitcher. With the hips already pointing away from the centerline toward the pitcher, the shift takes the weight outside the axis of the body (an imaginary vertical line extending from the head to the feet via the spine). Again, you lose balance.

Front-Foot Hitting

Many of the problems just described produce what is known as "front-foot hitting." These include "reaching for the ball" and "feeling for the ball." And when it comes to batting, these are big-time power outages!

Reaching for the ball is caused by swinging after the weight has partially or totally "leaked" forward. The swing is made almost exclusively with the arms and hands and with little use of the hips and legs. A good thought to combat this is "stay behind the ball."

Feeling for the ball happens when the batter's front leg is still bent at contact and after the swing. The batter is making contact with the ball but applying little or no force at impact. The batter's weight is completely off the backside and over the front leg, and the arms cannot reach full extension. As a result the overall swing and bat speed are slowed. This faulty swing is a bona fide ugly duckling.

Drills

Here are some drills to help you get from being slow, powerful, and ugly to fast, powerful, and beautiful (as in you're hanging out frozen ropes!).

- Have a parent, coach, or teammate throw you short tosses from about 30 feet. The focus of this drill is to allow each pitch to travel as far as possible before you take your cut. As the ball travels deep into the hitting zone, attack the ball with a short, direct swing and fast hip rotation. Hit the ball a bit earlier on inside strikes and a bit later on outside strikes. The object is to let the ball get as close as possible before swinging, or as Sarge said, "Let it travel, let it travel."
- Kneel on your back leg and extend your front leg straight toward the pitcher. Have someone soft-toss rolled-up socks to you from about 10 feet. This will train you to stay back on pitches, prevent a sloppy or excessive weight shift, and force you to call on your hip rotation to generate bat speed.

- During batting practice, devote an entire round to hitting the ball to the opposite field. Allow the pitches to travel deep into the strike zone and hit them as best as you can to the other side of the field. This will help you improve balance and control of your weight shift.

11

CUTTING YOUR SWING SHORT

You want to be as short to the ball as possible, with a long extension through the baseball. Keeping your bat moving through the ball after contact is what helps to get your entire body into hitting the ball.

—Mark McGwire

The baseball saying "short in the back and long in the front" applies not only to proper arm action among great pitchers but also to the swing among .300 hitters. A short, compact swing with a full follow-through gets results—and can win you a spot in the starting lineup.

"Short in the back" refers to an efficient movement of the bat to just in front of the rear shoulder, what is known as the batter's launch position. It shows early preparation and enables the batter to take a short, direct path to the ball. Batters can take many routes to the launch position. Some hold the bat straight up and down and directly in front of the chest, nearly motionless, and then glide it gently back to the launch position. Others hold it overhead and above the rear shoulder and then drop it down to the launch position. All of these movements have one thing in common—they are short in distance to the launch position and arrive there in plenty of time to "do some business," that is, attack the pitched ball.

"Long in the front" indicates that the batter has moved the arms to nearly full or full extension. This provides the fastest and most powerful delivery of the bat barrel to impact and through the hitting zone.

Mark McGwire made great strides as a power hitter when he shortened his swing in the back and lengthened it in the front. Early in his major-league career McGwire moved his hands and arms farther to the rear when he started his swing. Later, he cut down this movement to make his swing more compact and explosive. He also extended his arms throughout and past the point of contact. In effect, he became "long in the front" during and after contact.

Any arm action during the swing that cuts short the arc of the swing is a flaw. Here are some signs that indicate you are cutting your swing too short:

- Hitting balls weakly and failing to drive balls deep into the outfield
- Hitting balls exclusively to the pull side of the field
- Hitting high strikes on the ground or with topspin
- Hitting with a swing that resembles a "poking" rather than a "whipping" action

These are just a few of the symptoms of a shortened swing and follow-through. When you shorten your swing, you roll the top hand over the bottom hand too soon. This causes the bottom-hand arm to fold at the elbow, thus shortening the arc and power of the

Full extension of the arms: the top hand rolls over the bottom hand well after contact with the ball.

swing. A shortened arc slows the speed of the bat. The early or pre-mature top-hand action causes you to strike the top part of the ball, thus hitting grounders instead of line drives and long fly balls. In effect, you take the bat off the plane it must travel to meet the ball squarely and solidly at impact.

Extend, Extend, Extend

In a proper baseball swing, the bottom-hand arm starts slightly bent at the elbow in the stance and launch position. It first moves downward and forward and then begins to straighten as the bat moves from the launch position to impact. It reaches full extension either just beyond impact or at impact, but rarely before impact. The latter can happen but not by design, such as when you are fooled by an off-speed pitch and strike the ball well out in front of the plate.

74

When a swing is cut short the arms fail to extend.

The top-hand arm also straightens bit by bit throughout the swing. It reaches full extension at impact or slightly beyond impact. Look for a triangle formed with the shoulders and arms. If both arms are fully extended before impact, or if the top hand has left the bat and you're swinging with one hand (the bottom hand), you've been fooled with an off-speed pitch or you've got a bad case of lunging for the ball.

The top hand supplies more power and direction than the bottom hand. It literally propels the barrel of the bat to the ball. The bottom hand helps to guide the bat by pulling it through the zone as an upper-body extension of the rotating hips. But the top hand is the leader of the smack.

The top hand must propel the barrel full-throttle toward the incoming pitch, but it must not: (1) roll over too soon or (2) travel in a shortened (less powerful and slower) arc.

At impact the palm of the top hand is facing up and the palm of the bottom hand is facing down.

Drills

Allowing the top hand to dominate your swing often results in a swing that is too short. The top-hand action is flawed when it rolls the head of the bat over—and out of the swing plane or path needed to meet the ball squarely. Here are a couple of drills to promote better coordination of the hands, arms, and hips when swinging the bat through the impact area.

- Set a ball on a batting tee. Grip the bat with the bottom hand only, choking up six to eight inches. Extend your arm so that the bat is perpendicular to an imaginary line from the pitcher's mound to the plate. Face your palm down. Draw the bat back to your launch position, keeping only one hand on the handle. Next, deliver a short, direct blow to the back of the ball. Try to drive it straight toward the imaginary pitcher. Continue the movement of your arm until it is fully extended. Repeat 25 times.

  Re-grip the bat handle with both hands and place the bat just behind the ball, parallel to the ground, the hands in the palm-up, palm-down position. Repeat the remainder of the drill as previously described for 25 repetitions, trying to drive the ball to the back of the batting cage.

  After several sessions with the tee, repeat the drill with a partner pitching you soft tosses.
- With a partner providing soft tosses, take normal swings but stop moving your hands forward upon contact. Do not roll or snap your wrists—keep them in the palm-up, palm-down position. This allows you to feel the position your hands should be in at contact. Repeat 25 times.

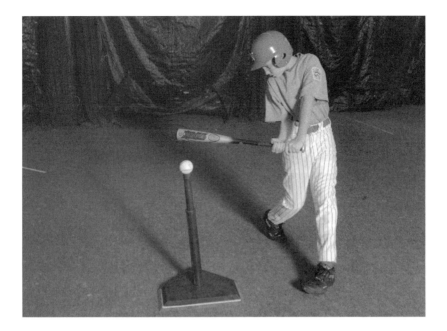

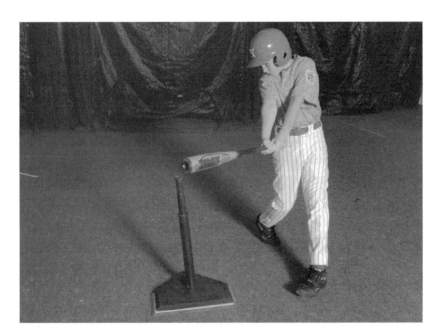

At impact the lead arm is closer to full extension than the top-hand arm (top). Just beyond impact both arms move to full extension (bottom).

12

NO SEPARATION

> It's very important to get something moving back before you start your swing forward. In our business it's called loading, and it's just like a prizefighter loading to throw a punch. By moving back first you'll generate more power.
>
> —Will Clark

All the great hitters and hitting instructors recognize that good hitters have some kind of loading action in their swings. They either shift their weight onto their back leg or coil their hip or front knee and hip, which brings the weight to the rear, or they turn the front hip and shoulder toward the plate by moving the hands back and up slightly in what is known as separation. Hitting guru Charley Lau recognized this when he said, "You've got to go back in order to go forward."

An important key to mastering proper hitting technique when coiling or shifting the weight onto the back leg is to momentarily keep the hands back as you step forward. This puts the hands in a position that is slightly separated from the body yet ready to strike at a pitch.

Coiling of the knee is a way to get rhythm and movement into the early stages of the swing and to start loading the swing with the big muscles of the legs and torso.

As you might guess, separation is a tricky concept in hitting because batters can get to this position in different ways. If you do not use a pronounced coiling or weight shift prior to swinging, the hands separate as you begin your step with the stride foot toward the pitcher. This produces a coiling action or weight shift that is a much quieter, less perceptible movement. However, it always results in a slight separation of the hands from the rear shoulder.

On the other hand, if you employ a bigger coil or shifting of weight onto the rear leg then the hands have already moved significantly to the rear. In this case, they have no need to go farther back, which would only get them trapped too far behind the launch position and cause them to travel too far to impact. In this case, simply keep them back—ready to swing the bat—as you stride toward the pitcher.

So, whether you use a coil, loading action, or a slight turn of the hips and shoulder, you must separate the hands slightly from the rear shoulder as you step forward toward the pitcher with your front (or stride) foot.

Signs of Poor Separation Technique

Here are a few clues to look for when troubleshooting this flaw:

- Batters will carry the upper body forward with the stride. This fails to produce a separation of the hands from the body's core and makes it impossible to fire the barrel of the bat in the split second that is required to recognize a pitch and decide to swing. Carrying the upper body forward with the stride step also moves too much weight too soon onto and directly over the front or stride foot.
- Poor separation also results in batters pushing the barrel of the bat into the path of the ball. This cuts down the speed of the swing and produces weakly hit balls.
- Batters will cut short the swing and finish without any extension of the arms.

To properly separate the hands when swinging, move the hands and bat handle slightly back and up three or four inches and at the same time take a short stride forward, perhaps no more than six inches, with the toe closed and the heel off the ground. Keep the hands back at shoulder height or slightly higher—whatever feels most comfortable. When the pitch is thrown:

1. First identify its speed and arc.
2. If you decide to swing, drop the heel of the stride foot and shift the weight onto the front leg.
3. Quickly rotate the hips and shoulders, bringing the arms and hands through the hitting or impact zone.

Pushing the barrel of the bat into the path of the ball produces weakly batted balls. Two telltale signs of this flaw are when the player (1) keeps the arms bent at the elbow throughout the swing and (2) moves the head too far forward—that is, too close to the contact point of the bat and the ball. When the correct technique is used, the arms move to full extension (elbows lock and arms extend) just past impact and the head moves slightly forward, stops, and remains back or behind the ball at contact.

Don't Trap the Hands

The separation of the hands can go wrong when you move them too far and get them "trapped" behind the shoulders. That is, they are so far back that they cannot reach the hitting point in time for the bat to meet the ball.

Some players, such as Ken Griffey, Jr., move their hands farther behind when they couple the separation with a backward rotation of their entire upper body. However, they keep their hands in the same position relative to the rear shoulder. They do not move them so far behind the rear shoulder that they would then fail to reach the hitting zone in time.

Other hitters turn their shoulders away much less from the pitcher. Their separation of the hands is more to the rear and less

If you move your hands too far behind the rear shoulder you will get them "trapped"—that is, so far to the rear that you cannot move back to the hitting area quick enough to meet the ball.

back and around like Griffey. Players such as Griffey who add coiling away from the pitcher in the separation phase of hitting have exceptionally strong back and abdominal muscles, which control the coiling and uncoiling.

Drill

Stand in front of a mirror in your normal stance. Practice "hiding your hands," that is, moving them until they're out of sight. This should position them slightly to the rear of the back shoulder. Done properly, this will also help in keeping your front shoulder and hips closed until you start your swing. As you move the hands to the rear take a short, soft stride with your toe closed (your foot should be nearly perpendicular to the imaginary pitcher). Plant your foot

"Hiding the hands"—that is, moving the hands to the launch position and partially out of the view of the pitcher as you stride—is a good way to help keep them back where they can "do some business."

as if you're stepping on eggshells, or testing ice on a lake for safety. Finally, drop your heel and transfer the weight to the front leg as you bring the bat through the impact area. Do this drill 20 to 30 times a day, 15 without swinging and 15 coupled with a swing. This will train you to get your body in the proper position for attacking the pitch.

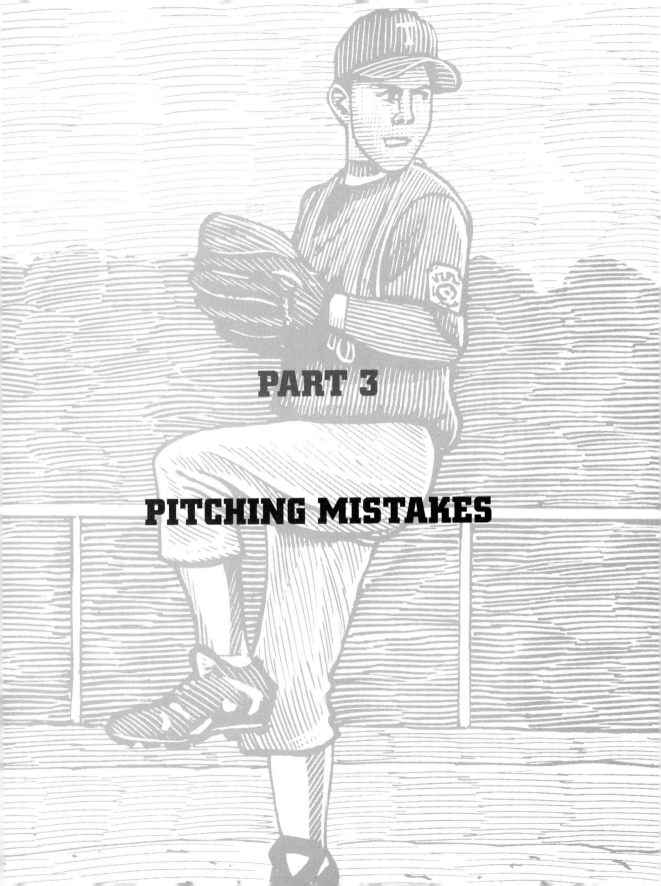

PART 3

PITCHING MISTAKES

13

NO BALANCE OVER THE RUBBER

A pitcher's head should never come off the imaginary vertical line from his pivot foot. In fact, the only time the head should ever be behind the rubber is when the pitcher is picking up the resin.

—Tom House, former major-league pitcher and pitching coach

Tom House's advice calls attention to your head, but the real issue that he is addressing is balance: balance when taking the sign while standing on the rubber, balance when taking the rocker step, and balance when posting over the pivot foot. Too many young pitchers display loss of balance in one or more of these pitching positions. Sometimes these flaws are the result of lack of leg or torso strength, but more often it is lack of understanding or execution of the proper mechanics or pitching techniques. The following discussion will help you to put and keep balance in your pitching delivery.

First let's take a look at how to maintain balance on the rubber before beginning your delivery, such as when you are taking the sign from the catcher. Our discussion will answer the following key questions: (1) Where do you put your feet? (2) How do you place them? (3) Should they be aligned directly alongside each other? (4) Should one be in front of the rubber and one in the back? (5) Should the weight be evenly distributed or on the balls of the feet?

Correct Stance

Spread your feet apart, up to shoulder width, with both feet pointing toward the plate. The stride foot (left foot for a right-handed pitcher) should be slightly to the rear of the plant or pivot foot (right foot for a right-handed pitcher), perhaps a few inches back with the heel slightly off the ground. As you begin your delivery, this will allow you to bring your weight back in a short "rocker step" before you bring it forward. This simple rocking motion is similar to what many hitters do. (Hitting requires balance too, so you will find some surprising similarities between striding to throw a baseball and striding to hit one.)

90

Place the arch of your pivot foot on the plate-side edge of the rubber with the toes and ball of your foot over the front edge. This

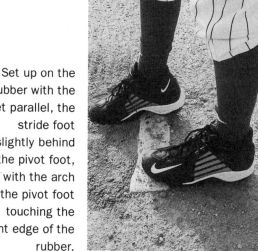

Set up on the rubber with the feet parallel, the stride foot slightly behind the pivot foot, and with the arch of the pivot foot touching the front edge of the rubber.

should give you a slight lean toward home plate and help avoid a flat-footed stance. When you begin your delivery, you will be pivoting off the rubber and placing this foot in front of and parallel to it. The only way to easily do this is with the toes and ball of your foot already in front of the rubber.

Keep your weight forward of the rubber (remember Tom House's advice about how often a pitcher's head should *ever* be

The rocker step is a short step back at a 45-degree angle. This starts the pitching motion and allows you to lift your pivot foot and place it in front of and parallel to the rubber.

Keep the head forward in a comfortable position when taking the rocker step.

behind the rubber) with the legs slightly flexed, head up, and eyes focused on the catcher and home plate.

Balance During the Rocker Step

The first pitching movement from the windup position is a rocker step, a soft and short step backward at a 45-degree angle taken with your stride foot or rear foot (the foot that is only partially touching the rubber when you're relaxed on the rubber taking the sign). Keep your head forward over the pivot foot and centered over the body. When the weight is centered you can maintain proper balance and you are positioned to exercise good body control.

Balance yourself over the posting leg and lift the knee with the toe pointed down until the thigh is parallel to the ground. This is the position in which you gather yourself briefly before delivering the pitch.

92

Shift your weight back and onto the stride foot (back foot), lift your pivot foot off the front edge of the rubber, turn it so it is parallel to the rubber, and drop it in front of the rubber. It should now be perpendicular to an imaginary line to home plate. Shift your weight onto the pivot foot and posting leg.

It is easy to lose balance while posting over the one leg, but you won't if you closely follow these simple movements. First, lift the knee of your lead or striding leg, letting the foot hang straight down from the knee. Do not swing the toe of the foot up and do not swing the knee to the side in an arc. Lift the knee straight up.

Here's how to check your balance. If you can stop and hold this position—that is, with your stride leg bent at the knee and hands folded together at the chest—you're perfectly balanced and "good to go." Some pitchers, such as Nolan Ryan or Orlando Hernandez, a.k.a. El Duque, can lift the lead knee up to the chest area and still maintain good balance in this posting position.

Here's how to finish off the posting position in a fully balanced movement. As you lift the knee, rotate the front hip closed to at least a 90-degree angle so that your front knee is pointing toward third base (for a right-handed pitcher). Maintain balance until the stride leg starts to lower. Do not drift forward early or tilt back toward first base.

Building Balance and Leg Strength

This exercise is relatively easy and a lot of fun. Try doing it with a buddy and competing to see who can perform the movements without losing balance.

Stand with your feet together, hands and arms outstretched to the sides. Lift your left leg (if you are a right-handed pitcher) until your thigh is parallel and lower leg is perpendicular to the ground. Maintain perfect balance while holding this position for a count of 15; then lower your leg. Repeat the leg lift; then straighten the leg so that it is parallel to the ground. Hold for a count of 15. Repeat with the leg bent at the knee; then rotate your hips and shoulders to the right as far as possible, maintaining balance. Hold for a count of 15. Repeat with your leg straightened and hold for a count of 15.

Lift your knee until the thigh is parallel to the ground. Extend your arms and hold this position for a count of 15 seconds. Start with two sets of 10 reps daily.

Hold the posting position with your arms against your body (top). Extend the leg to create a different center of gravity (bottom), which will improve balance. Mix this into your practice drills (but not into your pitching motion).

From the posting position (top), turn away from the target and hold for a count of 15 seconds (bottom). Do two sets of 10 reps daily.

14

FINGERS UNDER THE BALL

> *Don't get too fancy with grips. Master one first. It should lie firmly in your hand, and yet if someone firmly tapped the ball, it would fall out.*
>
> —Tom Seaver

The problem of placing the fingers under the ball is common to many Little League players, especially pitchers who have small hands and fingers. Because their short fingers do not wrap sufficiently around the ball, they compensate by placing their fingers under the ball. Even the official Little League baseball, which has a slightly smaller circumference than a major-league ball, is difficult for some young players to grasp properly.

In addition, younger players often do not have adequate hand strength to make a proper grip. Thus, they cannot grip the ball firmly enough to exert sufficient pressure on the ball in the pads of the fingers and thumb. To compensate, they grip the ball farther back into the palm or place their hand under the ball (to support it), all of which creates pitch-release and velocity problems.

It is better to grip the ball with the pads and tips of the fingers (background), not in the palm (foreground). Young players with small hands have difficulty with the proper grip.

98

Staying on Top

To pitch effectively and to throw strikes consistently, you must learn to keep your first two fingers on top of and directly behind the ball. In prescribing the correct way to grip and throw a pitch, we're limiting the remarks to a four-seam fastball (which is gripped across the seams at their widest point).

First grip the ball across the wide seams (they form a horseshoe) placing the finger pads on the seams. For younger players, the fingers should be one-quarter to one-half of an inch apart. To improve control, you may spread the fingers apart slightly.

Keep the fingers on top of and behind the ball.

Grip the ball across the seams, with the ball resting on the first pad of the thumb between the center of the pad and the nail.

Place the thumb directly under the ball and fingers, with the ball resting on the pad of the first joint about halfway between the center of the pad and the nail. Do not place the ball in the middle of

the fleshy pad of the thumb but rather alongside the pad along the bonier area next to the nail. To check the thumb's positioning, remove the ball after placing it underneath the fingers and above the thumb and observe where the pad of the thumb is facing. If placed properly it should be directly facing the fourth finger, not either of the fingers gripping the ball across the top. This allows the thumb to drop out from under

To check the proper alignment of the fingers and thumb, turn the hand palm-side up (top), remove the ball without moving the placement of the fingers and thumb (bottom left), and then bend the thumb (bottom right). It should intercept the fourth finger.

HIGH ELBOW EQUALS LOW STRIKES

Pitching coaches agree that throwing a baseball is a high-elbow skill, that is, you must raise the elbow of your throwing arm to shoulder height when bringing it forward to the release point. The elbow must stay close to the midline of the body while the throwing hand moves slightly away from the midline (for a right-handed pitcher, closer to the third-base line).

When you raise the elbow you create a better angle of the trajectory of the ball from the release point to the target. When your stride foot strikes the ground your throwing arm should have reached shoulder height, forming an angle of 90 degrees between the forearm and shoulder. Keep this angle until the torso rotates and you must release the ball. Keeping the 90-degree angle reduces stress on the throwing arm.

If you fail to raise the elbow, you will put undue stress on the front side of the throwing shoulder and the inside of the throwing elbow. It also will result in consistently high pitches—a no-no in any league.

Grip the ball in the fingertips and keep the wrist relaxed and flexible.

the ball as it rolls off the middle finger during its release.

The ring finger is flexed toward the palm (remember that smaller fingers will not fold entirely into the palm), with the inside of the finger—between the first and second knuckle joints—contacting the ball. The pinky finger is alongside the ring finger and has no direct role in the grip.

Hold the ball out toward the end of the fingers and back toward the palm (it does not contact the fleshy part of the palm). Apply light grip pressure with the pads of the two fingers and thumb. Keep the wrist joint loose and forearm muscles relaxed.

Releasing the Pitch

Face the palm of the hand toward home plate, with the first two fingers on top of and directly behind the ball. Bring the arm forward. As the arm and hand cross a line about even with the pitcher's face, flex the wrist forward. Drop the thumb slightly, flex the fingers forward, and follow the ball toward the target. The arm and wrist will pronate (the palm will face to the outside of the body). The ball will roll off the middle finger last and rotate toward the target with the four seams spinning. On the follow-through, continue to bring the arm down, across the body, and over the outside of the lead leg or stride leg.

When releasing the ball, the wrist and hand should be closer to the third-base line than the elbow.

Drill

Stand in the posting position with the hands held together on the upper chest slightly higher than the letters and just below the base of the neck. Place the throwing hand inside the pocket of the glove, with the glove's fingers facing away from home plate. Position the first and middle finger of the throwing hand on top of the ball and the thumb underneath.

Using a controlled fall toward the plate, gradually drop the stride leg while keeping the back elbow (throwing arm), back shoulder, front shoulder, and lead elbow horizontal to the ground and the body aligned directly to the plate. As you fall break the hands, moving the throwing hand down slightly and to the rear, showing the ball to the center fielder. Raise the throwing-arm elbow up to shoulder level, with the forearm and elbow forming a 90-degree angle aligned directly to the plate. Step toward the plate with the stride foot, landing on the balls of the stride foot as the throwing arm reaches the 90-degree angle.

Repeat 10 times under the watchful eye of a teammate, coach, or parent.

Keep your hands higher up on the chest when posting.

Bring the ball down, back, and up and show it to the center fielder (top).
Keep the elbow at shoulder height (bottom).

15

RUSHING YOUR DELIVERY TO THE PLATE

> *Driving your left arm down outside your left hip . . . as though you were trying to knock the wind out of someone behind you, will help establish good off-arm (glove-side) mechanics. Pulling with your hand rather than your elbow will cause you to sling the ball.*
>
> —Tom Seaver

Pitchers who sling the ball are also guilty of rushing to the plate, of rotating open the glove-hand side too soon—long before the throwing hand is in position. When a pitcher moves toward the plate too soon, that is, before the throwing hand has moved down, back, and up so that the elbow is at shoulder height when the body begins to bend over the leg of the stride foot, that pitcher is said to be "rushing." Failing to synchronize the upper and lower body movements causes the pitcher to release the ball at a point behind, rather than over, the stride foot. This flaw in the delivery often results in loss of control high and out of the strike zone.

A close relative of rushing in the family of pitching flaws is when a pitcher steps too far to the glove-hand side when making the stride and throw. For our discussion, this mechanical error is called "stride-aside." When in this position the torso of the body cannot rotate and bend properly, if at all, and this makes it impossible for the pitcher to maintain a consistent release point. This also puts a tremendous strain on the shoulder and arm muscles and often results in injuries.

Most rushing and stride-aside problems are caused by the pitcher's failure to stop, or pause, momentarily at the conclusion of the leg raise. This momentary gathering of the limbs and arms close to the body is the pause position, and it is an essential element of any sound delivery.

The pause position is the first moment of truth in the delivery. It is here that all the preliminary movements—rocker step, pivot, posting over the pivot foot, raising of the stride leg—are concluded, and the body is prepared to move toward the plate. It is a position

You should be balanced when in the correct pause or gathering position.

of control and balance from which the pitcher will move powerfully and efficiently.

Here's what the correct pause position looks like: The hands are together, pressed gently against the middle of the chest, and all the body weight is centered over and supported by the pivot leg. (A pitcher should be able to stay balanced in this position indefinitely. If he cannot, his weight is either too far forward or backward.) The pitcher stops in the pause position in order to consolidate and control the power that he loaded with the pivot and leg raise. When practicing the pause position, it may be helpful to have the pitcher count "one, one thousand" before moving toward home plate. Remember, this applies only to the pause position in the full windup and not the set position, which you will use when you move on from Little League baseball.

A common mistake is to point the toe of the stride foot skyward and to lean toward right field. This position makes it hard to stride consistently.

The correct way to move the stride leg into the pause position is to raise the knee straight up, toes pointed down. However, there is room for your own individual movement as long as it does not destroy control and balance of your body. Orlando "El Duque" Hernandez and Hall of Fame pitcher Nolan Ryan bring their knees to the upper chest, while future Hall of Famer Greg Maddux uses a relatively low leg raise. The most important thing is that each unique position works.

Just prior to moving toward home plate the stride foot should be under the knee in a relaxed position. Keep the toes pointed toward the ground. Do not permit the toes to point toward the sky. This often produces a heel landing, which causes not only a loss of balance and control but also an inconsistent release point.

The first movement from the pause position is critical because it involves two simultaneous actions: (1) slowly break the hands—that is, remove the ball from the glove with the throwing hand—and (2) lower the leg as you drift toward the plate with your lead leg and stride foot. The throwing hand goes down, back, and up toward the cocked position in a continuous motion.

As you drift extend the lead elbow toward the plate. Drift downward until you plant the stride foot. Then pull the lead elbow down and alongside the lead hip, which is opened—that is, facing toward home plate. Then rotate the trunk or torso swiftly to square the hips. After squaring the hips bend the torso forward and down, flexing from the waist over a braced stride leg.

As the lead foot plants, the upper body and head remain at the top center of a widening triangle of the body (when viewed from the side). The body does not sit down, it does not leap or jump itself forward in a rush. Rather, it moves forward unhurriedly and without hesitation, and stabilizes over the lead or front foot, which has formed a flexed position at approximately a 135-degree angle. You are now ready to turn on the power.

Move from the posting position by breaking the hands and drifting toward home plate. Keep the throwing-arm elbow up and the shoulders aligned toward the target, with the lead shoulder pointing at the catcher's mitt (top). Pull down with the lead elbow (bottom).

Pull the lead elbow down alongside the lead hip.

Keep the hand and wrist closer to the throwing-hand-side baseline (third-base line for a right-handed pitcher) than the elbow.

Where are the arm and hand when the body is at its maximum torque? Upon stride-foot contact, the pitching hand should be approximately cap-high, and the hand should be slightly closer to the throwing-hand-side baseline than the elbow. The release point—that is, when the ball leaves the hand—occurs as the hand passes by the stride foot. The fingers are behind and on top of the ball.

16

INCORRECT PLACEMENT OF THE STRIDE FOOT

Throwing starts with the feet and sequences through the legs, torso, arms, and finally the baseball.

—Tom House, major-league pitching coach

The stride foot is very important in several parts of the pitching delivery. It initiates the delivery with the rocker step, or step back when you're just getting started. It helps the pitcher gather momentum when the stride foot and knee are lifted toward the chest. And it positions the body for the hip turn just prior to release of the ball.

The most common mistake that young pitchers make with the stride foot is placing it in the wrong position when stepping toward home plate. But what is the correct position? To correctly place the stride foot, land it flat, weight on the ball of the foot, on a straight line toward the target with the toes slightly closed. This allows you to rotate the hips and bend the back over the leg of the stride foot. As a rule of thumb, a pitcher is striding incorrectly when the stride foot lands two or more inches off the imaginary line from the rubber to home plate.

Stepping too far to either side of the imaginary line will get you into trouble. If you step too far toward the first-base side (for a right-handed pitcher) of the imaginary line you will bring on several problems. The first is that you will place tremendous, unnecessary stress on the shoulder muscles. This can lead to serious injury, including tears of the rotator-cuff muscles.

The second problem is lack of control. You will not be able to consistently make your delivery at the same arm angle or arm slot, that is, the arm's path and point of release. Without a consistent release point you cannot consistently throw pitches that hit the target.

Another equally important problem that comes with a misplaced stride is that you will not throw with high velocity. Without the aid

The correct stride is directly toward the target.

of the more powerful leg, torso, and upper and lower back muscles—whose power cannot be fully harnessed with a stride so far to the one side—you cannot bring the heat.

In a nutshell, here's why. The motion of throwing a baseball is much like the motion of a whip that is cracked. When you crack a whip, the farthest end of the whip, which is like the fingertips of your throwing arm, moves at an incredible rate of speed (as fast as the speed of sound). When you throw a baseball, the arm action works under the same law of physics that explains why the tip of the whip speeds up when it is cracked. This law allows for the momentum that is generated at the beginning of the rotation around your hips to feed into the very end of your arm, that is, the hand and fingertips. This increases the speed of the wrist action and hand in the very last stages of the forward throwing motion and release of the ball.

A common mistake is to stride "closed"—too far to the pitcher's throwing-hand side.

When you stride too far to the left (for a right-handed pitcher), you open your hips too soon and are unable to conserve and build momentum to be transferred into the throwing hand. It's true that the hips rotate somewhat, but not nearly enough to build the necessary hand and arm speed for above-average fastballs.

Many times this fault is caused by improper balance and weight transfer during the stride, and by not closing up the hips and shoulders during the leg lift. This can be a difficult fault to correct because many Little League players have not yet developed abdominal and hip muscles that are strong enough to close up or rotate their trunk to stride correctly. One drill that can help is to stand on the posting leg, hands across the chest, lift the leg, and turn to the right. Hold this for 15 seconds. Do 15 repetitions. Repeat with hands held to the side and the leg extended.

A common mistake is to stride "open"—too far to the pitcher's glove side.

Closed Stride

Striding too far to the right of the imaginary line, that is, toward the third-base side for a right-handed pitcher, also causes control problems. Coaches often call this mechanical mistake "throwing across your body." This is aptly named because the pitcher sweeps the arm across the entire front of the body from the shoulder to the waist. Instead, the pitcher should be bringing the arm down and to the outside of the stride leg, not high and straight across the body.

If you are consistently throwing balls high and to the right (for a right-handed pitcher) this might be your problem. If you are leaving your breaking balls up in the zone, or having trouble getting good rotation and movement on your breaking balls, the solution to this problem might start with the stride.

Drill

Draw a chalk line from a midpoint on the rubber to the middle of home plate. Place your toe so that the midpoint of the rubber is alongside the outside of the foot of your posting leg. Take your windup and rocker step, lifting and placing the foot of your posting leg in front of and alongside the rubber so that the toes touch the chalk line, and then stride directly toward home plate. Land your stride foot on the chalk line. You can also practice the stride in front of a mirror. Repeat a dozen times.

17

MISALIGNMENT OF THE SHOULDERS AND ARMS

> *I often see young pitchers dawdle in getting the ball out of the glove. They forget that a key to effective pitching is rapid, coordinated movement of the hands from the glove through the backswing to the release point to the plate. "Get it out and get up."*
>
> —Tom Seaver

Misaligning the shoulders and arms when striding forward is the cause of many problems in the delivery of young pitchers. When the shoulders and arms are not aligned, (1) the arm slot or position where the ball is released changes constantly, (2) hand speed is slowed, and (3) deception is lost.

The shoulders and arms are misaligned when they do not form a straight line toward home plate as the stride foot moves forward toward its landing spot. This flaw can be most easily detected from the rear of the pitcher or from the front standing behind the catcher. Viewed from behind home plate, a misaligned delivery will show the shoulders angled toward the third-base line and the throwing hand pointing toward right field (for a right-handed

The shoulders are perpendicular to the direction of the stride at the start (top), aligned during the stride (bottom), and rotating during the delivery of the pitch (opposite).

pitcher). The throwing hand may be either very high or very low—both are faults that need to be addressed.

Proper Alignment

When the landing foot hits the ground (weight taken on the balls of the foot), keep your lead-arm elbow, front shoulder, rear shoulder, and throwing-arm elbow in line with the home plate target. Form a straight line from the foot of the posting leg to the foot of the stride leg.

Keep the elbows at least at shoulder height, with the throwing elbow bent at 90 degrees. Point your lead-arm elbow toward home plate and then drive it downward as you bring the throwing arm up to the cocked position (90-degree angle formed by the elbow and forearm). This position will enable you to consistently bring the ball forward every time to the same release point—what we call the "arm slot." Maintaining a consistent arm slot is a key to con-

A common flaw for a right-handed pitcher is to angle the shoulders toward the right-field side of second base.

trol and command of your pitches. See the accompanying sidebar for comments by Hall of Fame pitcher Tom Seaver on the importance of grooving this release point in your delivery.

This alignment is also a key to building hand speed for the delivery. The torso and arms move around an axis—your spine—when you rotate the hips. The momentum generated by the rotation around the axis is eventually fed into your arm and hand.

Proper alignment also aids in creating deception among hitters. When viewed by the hitter, the lead-arm elbow, forearm, and glove hide the hitter's view of your throwing arm. Work to give the hitter a view of your throwing arm and the ball as late as possible in the delivery. Hitters are trained to pick up the ball as early as possible because the earlier they detect the pitch the more time they have to identify the pitch and react. So avoid a poor positioning of

TOM SEAVER'S ADVICE ON GETTING THE THROWING-ARM ELBOW UP AND RELEASE POINT

"Your [throwing-arm] elbow must be above your shoulder to insure that you achieve the downward plane through the strike zone. Aim to establish a 45-degree angle from the release point . . . to your follow-through point.

"You must work constantly to perfect the exact release point. If you are too close to your ear [when you bring the ball forward during the throwing arc], your hand may be on the inside part of the ball instead of on top of it. If your hand is too far outside your ear [for a right-handed pitcher, too much toward the third-base line], you run the risk of gripping and throwing the ball from the outside instead of on top. You must stay on top of the ball and maintain an angle approaching 45 degrees downward. There will, of course, be individual variations in obtaining the optimum release points."

—from *The Art of Pitching*, by Tom Seaver

123

the arms. For example, don't show the ball early by slinging it out behind your back and then bringing it around in a measurably slower throwing arc.

Poor arm positioning not only risks injury, it upsets the balance during your delivery. Slinging the throwing arm down, back, and away from the body during the stride moves the center of gravity outside the torso and knee of the stride leg. Lost balance and poor control result.

Drill

Stand with your back to a wall or chain-link fence, heels parallel about six inches from the wall or fence. Assume the posting position. Simultaneously break the hands and take a step forward with the stride foot. If you misalign your arms, shoulders, glove hand, or throwing hand you will hit the wall or fence. Practice until you can make this move without brushing the wall or fence.

Establishing an effective release angle will require devoted individual effort. But you cannot go wrong if you follow these basic principles: keep your fingers on top of the ball; keep your elbow above your shoulders; and bring your arm down at a 45-degree angle toward your opposite hip (down and outside the stride leg).

A common flaw is to release the ball too close to the head.

Another common flaw is to release the ball with the fingers alongside instead of on top of the ball.

Experiment with different release points. Work with your coach. Ask for opinions on whether you are maintaining the same (or very nearly the same) release point.

18

LACK OF TRUNK ROTATION

Hip rotation is very important to maximize your velocity. If you look at most of your hard throwers in the game, they have very well-developed thigh muscles and buttocks. You've got to have a strong lower half to throw hard. They go hand in hand.

—Mel Queen, major-league pitching coach

Unfortunately, this problem causes a chain reaction of problems. It slows down pitch velocity, raises the risk of injury to the shoulder muscles, ruins control, and leaves the pitcher in a poor position to field batted balls. A delivery without trunk rotation is like a car without a drive train—there is no way to build and transfer energy to the ball. Let's take a closer look at this killer flaw.

Causes

Several factors are responsible for lack of trunk rotation. With young players it is often lack of strength in the hip and torso muscles, a condition that can be solved by only time and muscle growth. These big muscles are needed to move the upper body around the spine and to build arm and hand speed. Other factors that produce this flaw can be corrected with some drills. They are:

- Pushing off the rubber bent over and low, which looks like "diving into the pitch" to the observer
- Folding up the stride leg instead of bracing it so that it can serve as a post around which the hips rotate
- Stepping with the stride leg closed (too far to the right for a right-handed pitcher), which makes it impossible for the hips to fully rotate (the result is throwing weakly across the body)
- Overstriding, which prevents trunk flexion or bending over the flexed stride leg and produces balls thrown high in the zone

What Is Proper Trunk Rotation?

The stride and planting of the stride foot sets up hip rotation. The throwing arm, hand, and wrist are loaded, extended slightly back toward the pitcher's head and moving forward when the stride foot hits the ground. But the body stops moving forward when the front leg braces—the hips open slightly but the shoulders stay aligned slightly longer toward home plate. This bracing action of the front leg provides a firm base against which the upper body can rotate.

In rapid sequence, the hips open—that is, the right (for a right-handed pitcher), or trailing, hip moves around with the spin and squares alongside the left hip—and the torso and shoulders quickly square with the hips, creating tremendous torque (rotational force), much as the energy stored in a twisted rubber band. As the trunk or torso unwinds, springing from extension to flexion, and the shoulders square up with the hips, the head and shoulders move over the braced front leg. The body unleashes rotational forces as the shoulders square with the hips, and vertical or downward forces as the upper body flexes over the front leg. The result: tremendous arm and hand speed—thus, pitch velocity.

As the trunk and shoulder rotate and square off to the plate, the shoulder rotates externally with the elbow leading. The forearm and hand then fire forward, coming outside the elbow. As the trunk goes from extension (an arched back) to flexion (bending over the front leg), the arm and hand accelerate to the release point.

The release point—that is, when the ball leaves the hand—occurs as the hand passes by the stride foot. The fingers are behind and on top of the ball.

Follow-Through and Trunk Rotation

Lack of trunk rotation dramatically affects the follow-through. Proper follow-through prepares the pitcher to field batted balls.

Bring the hand down and over the stride leg during the follow-through.

With little or no trunk rotation you do not finish in a position that is square to the batter, the preferred position for reacting to any batted ball.

When you correctly rotate your hips you bring your throwing arm, hand, and shoulder down, over and outside the lead leg. This allows you to land square to the plate and bring your glove hand up and in front of your body—for protection and to be ready to field a ball batted directly at you. Even if your rotation pulls you slightly off balance, usually toward the first-base side of the field for a right-handed pitcher, you can take a short jump forward and get squared. Because Pedro Martinez's delivery involves an extreme rotation of the hips, he performs this move during the follow-through of his delivery.

To develop backside drive, practice bringing the back knee forward and inward and balance on the stride leg at the finish.

Drill

Here is a drill that will help you develop good rotation in your delivery. Play catch at half-speed with a teammate at 30 to 35 feet (keep the distance shorter than the official Little League pitching distance). Concentrate on pulling the back knee forward and inward and balancing on a braced stride leg. Keep the pivot foot suspended in the air and remain balanced for five seconds. This will not only improve hip rotation but build strength in the stride leg and develop backside drive, that is, bring the back knee forward and inward. Repeat 10 times.

PART 4

FIELDING MISTAKES

19

POOR SETUP POSITION BY INFIELDERS

An infielder must make his first move to his right or left, not forward or backward. In order to move laterally a player must have his weight distributed evenly on the balls of his feet. As the ball is released by the pitcher he should not be leaning forward or back but have his weight divided evenly on each foot.

—Earl Weaver

Fielding may be the most overlooked and least understood aspect of baseball, but it wasn't on the Baltimore Orioles teams of manager Earl Weaver. His 15 teams in the 1970s and early 1980s won 30 Gold Gloves and were first or second in fielding percentage every year. Team and individual preparation from the likes of third baseman Brooks Robinson, shortstop Mark Belanger, second baseman Bobby Grich, and others made the difference. These players set up properly on every pitch and made the plays day after day, season after season.

The Setup Position

Here are the elements of the correct setup position for infielders:

1. Stand with the feet slightly more than shoulder-width apart—this promotes balance and stability.
2. Flex the knees, bend at the waist—this provides flexibility, balance, and the quickness to spring in any direction.
3. Keep the weight on the balls of the feet—this promotes a quicker response and maintains balance.
4. Get the glove down, with the back of the glove's fingertips in the dirt—this allows you to be ready for hard-hit balls directly at you and keeps the body low and ready to react.
5. Lean forward as the pitcher releases the ball, move right or left when it's hit—learn to read the swing so you can anticipate which side you will first move toward.

When setting the feet, do not place them square to the front. Place them slightly off-line. For right-handed players, place the front of the right foot on an imaginary line that intercepts the arch of the left foot. For left-handed players (typically, first basemen), it's just the opposite. This foot alignment places the glove hand slightly forward of the body, which allows for easier maneuvering of the glove hand and a more natural removal of the ball from the glove when you must get off a throw.

Getting the Best Jump

Why is assuming the correct "ready" or setup position so important? The speed of the fielder's initial reaction toward the ball often determines whether you get to the ball in time to make the play. The quickest way to get the best jump on the ball is from the proper setup position, which enables the fielder to react quickly in any

Set up with your glove-side leg slightly forward of your throwing-side leg (top). A straight line parallel to your shoulders drawn on the ground would run from the toe of your right foot through the arch of your left foot (for a right-handed fielder). Look the ball into your glove when catching it (bottom).

direction. If you have your weight back on your heels, for example, you will not react as quickly toward a slowly hit ground ball.

Remember, when the batter hits the ball on the ground in the infield, it becomes a race. The infielder tries to field the ball cleanly and deliver it to first base before the batter arrives there. In this type of competition it is imperative that the infielder gain every possible advantage. The setup position is one of those advantages.

By using the proper setup position consistently throughout the game, you will be more likely to remain alert and avoid lapses of concentration. Many fans are attracted to baseball because of its leisurely pace. This easy tempo, however, is often interrupted by events that require players to be attentive and "into the game." Any

The first step from the setup position is either left, right, or forward. If you move to the left, quickly angle the left foot about 45 degrees (as shown) and push off with the right foot (for a right-handed fielder). The first step will then be the right foot crossing over to the left.

GREAT FIELDERS READ THE PITCHES

An important part of getting ready to move after a ball is hit is reading the pitch. Good infielders move after the ball has been hit. Great ones move before it has been hit.

Cal Ripken, Jr., did not have great speed afoot, yet he always managed to get to the balls hit his way when he played shortstop or third base. Ripken's ready stance included placing his feet slightly more than shoulder-width apart and gently lowering his glove, pocket facing the sky, to the ground as the ball crossed home plate. He did this while at the same time reading the pitch, that is, anticipating where the ball was going to be hit.

For example, if a hanging curveball or other off-speed pitch was thrown over the middle or inside of the plate to a right-handed pull hitter (who will open the hips and quickly get the barrel of the bat out in front of the plate where it contacts the ball), Ripken instinctively moved to his right. A fielder reacts differently when playing against a hitter who sprays the ball to all fields, someone like Tony Gwynn who can stay behind the ball and drive a pitch, especially one over the outside part of the plate, to the opposite field. In this situation, the fielder's anticipation is to break to the left (or right side of the diamond).

Focusing on the angle of the bat as it drives through the hitting zone is key in getting a jump on the ball. If the barrel of the bat is ahead of the hands, look for the ball to be pulled. If the hands are leading the barrel, look for a ball to go to the opposite field. If the hands and barrel arrive at the ball simultaneously, look for the ball up the middle.

mental lapses by fielders may result in critical mistakes that can affect the game's outcome. One method of maintaining alertness on the field is to consistently utilize the setup position. In this way, your body keeps your mind in the game.

Drill

Here is a drill that parents and coaches can do with a player. Ask the player to get in position in the infield to practice fielding ground balls. Before hitting each ground ball, make sure the fielder displays all the ingredients of the proper setup position. As you hit each ground ball, observe whether the setup position is maintained and if the player reacts quickly enough in the direction of the ball. If extra players are available, assign a designated runner to run from home plate to first base at the crack of the bat.

20

INFIELDER FIELDING THE BALL BACK UNDER THE LEGS

> When you catch the ball, you look it into your glove and watch as you take it out. You do all the basics. Then when the ball is hit, your athletic ability and reactions take over.
>
> —Barry Larkin

After an infielder moves toward a ground ball and gets down into the proper stance to catch the ball, he should look at the ball as it enters his glove and as he removes it to throw. The most efficient way to do this is by placing your glove low to the ground and extending your arms fully in front of your body. It is not uncommon to see a young player make the mistake of placing the glove between the legs or back under the legs. Although the glove may be low enough to the ground, the fingers are pointing downward, which can permit the ball to more easily fall out. This awkward position should be avoided. It can create several problems, including loss of balance and a delay in making the throw.

To correctly position yourself to field ground balls, lower your body by bending at the waist and legs and extending your hands out in front.

What's the Big Deal?

Let's look more closely at what difficulties can arise by fielding the ball back under the legs.

- You give the ball extra time to change its direction or take a bad hop.
- You momentarily lose sight of the ball because you cannot easily look the ball into your glove.
- The position of your glove and hands may cause you to lose balance or trip when you begin your footwork in preparation to throw.
- You waste time in the delivery process because it takes longer to get the ball to your chest and out of your glove. The sooner you get the ball into your glove, the sooner it comes out.
- You lose the softness in your hands and the feel for the ball.

A common mistake is to field the ball too far back and under the body.

Sweeping the Floor

Imagine you are cleaning up a mess on the floor using a dustpan and brush. You place the dustpan flat on the floor and extend it forward as the dirt is swept into the pan. Now, think of your glove as the dustpan and use this technique. Spread your legs a little more than shoulder-width apart and bend your knees. Place your glove down on the ground, fully opened (just like the dustpan). Extend your arms and glove fully forward in anticipation of the ball sweeping into your glove. Move your bare hand over the glove with the palm of the hand facing down toward the opened glove (this helps you control a ball that takes a bad hop and enables you to quickly remove the ball from the glove).

Next, scoop the ball by bringing the glove forward to meet the ball. Keep your hands "soft," that is, allow a little "give" as the ball

144

Catch an approaching ball by extending the hands forward low to the ground and watching it come into the glove.

enters the glove (think of gently catching a raw egg in your bare hands). Then raise both hands up to your chest in preparation to throw.

Always expect a ground ball to remain low and skim the ground, rather than anticipating a big hop. This will serve as a reminder to you to keep your glove low to the ground. Don't worry, you will be able to react easily to any ball that may happen to arrive at a higher level. If your body and glove start down low, you can quickly rise to meet a big hop. But it takes longer to go down to catch a low ball from a higher position.

Drill

Pair two players opposite each other, starting at about 10 feet apart. Draw a line in front of each player representing the length of the player's arm extension. Each player takes a turn rolling the ball to the other. The receiving player must extend the glove to the line when catching the ground ball, then bring both hands up to the chest. The feet should not move in this drill so as not to alter the player's distance from the line. The receiving player then rolls the ball to the other player, who is expected to do the same. The distance between the players and the velocity of the ground balls can increase during the drill.

Perfect Practice Makes Perfect Play

Batting practices conducted by most baseball teams often look alike. A coach throws pitches to a hitter at home plate. Two or three players wait their turn on deck, and everyone else takes positions in the field to catch balls hit by the batter. This can be boring and unproductive to most players in the field, but smart players can use it as a practice tool in overcoming poor fielding habits.

Let's look at a common double-play scenario to see how catching the ball out in front of your body can be of help to your fellow infielders as well as yourself. Picture shortstop Barry Larkin fielding a ground ball to his left to start a double play. The second baseman comes over to cover the bag, expecting a short shovel toss from Barry. Barry properly catches the ball out in front of his body, which accomplishes two things. First, it enables him to use his soft hands to scoop and cradle the ball into his glove and quickly remove it. It also allows the second baseman to see the ball in Barry's glove and follow it as it is removed and tossed to him. Barry is actually showing the ball to his second baseman from the instant he receives it. If Barry had fielded the ball back under his legs, the second baseman would have temporarily lost sight of the ball. Then he would have to find the ball again as it reappeared from between Barry's legs. Magic acts belong in the circus, not on the baseball field.

Here is what you can do. Take a position in the infield and wait for a ground ball to be hit in your direction. Rather than making a casual attempt to catch the ball, take the opportunity to improve your technique. If your habit is to catch ground balls between your legs instead of out in front, then take advantage of the "live" ball off the bat to practice correct technique. You can also ask a coach, friend, or family member to hit you ground balls whenever time permits. This will help to reinforce good habits that you have acquired. Major-league infielders take seemingly endless amounts of ground balls daily. That is why their fielding actions look so natural. What is their secret? They practice good fielding habits.

21

INFIELDER'S FAILURE TO MOVE THE BODY IN FRONT OF THE BALL

The great plays are made because your fundamentals are sound.

—Barry Larkin

As a fielder, you want to give yourself the best opportunity to catch the ball. If you don't move quickly enough to get your body centered on the ball as it arrives, you're not helping yourself. Of course, ground balls hit too far to either side of you are the exceptions. But for any balls hit in your range, you owe it to yourself and your team to put all your energy into making the play correctly. All you need to do is pay attention to fundamentals and exert the necessary energy.

Imagine a vertical line drawn on your body from your nose down to your belly button. That is your center—where you have the best chance of catching the ball. If a bad hop occurs, your body is also in the best position to block it. Anything off-center may result in the ball bouncing to your side and away from you. If you block the ball, you may still have time to throw the runner out or make the play. Just move your body over the ball and pick it up with your bare hand—not with your glove. You will get a better grip on the ball and release the ball quicker using the bare hand.

Technique plus Energy

Getting your body squarely in front of the ball involves several steps. When the ball is hit, get a good jump and charge the ball. You need quick feet. Lazy feet result in backhand plays. Don't settle for doing it the hard way. All it takes is a quick burst of energy. Always move forward—even on a hard-hit ball where you may only be able to move in a step or two. You never want to catch a ball flat-footed or back on your heels. Keep your eyes focused on the ball. Keep your body low to the ground and knees bent. Standing upright will keep your weight too far back and cause you to lose balance. Take shorter steps as you get close to the ball so you can

Use your bare hand to help capture the ball, secure it, and remove it quickly from the pocket for the throw.

time your arrival to get your preferred hop. Never let the ball
determine your hop. That's your
job. And create an angle toward
the target that reduces the distance and creates momentum in
that direction.

Begin the crossover step by pivoting open toward the direction you will move.

Sometimes you'll need to move
laterally first. Use the crossover
step to get to your right or left the
quickest. For example, for a right-
handed player, if the ball is hit to
your left, cross over with your
right foot while pivoting on the
ball of your left foot. If it is hit to your right, cross over with your
left foot while pivoting on your right foot. Always try to get in front
of the ball on these plays rather than settling for the backhand. It
gives you the best chance of making the play because you'll be well
balanced, which will help you catch the ball cleanly and throw the
ball harder and more accurately. As always, the simple method is
the most efficient.

149

Maintaining your concentration is a must. Follow the pitch in to
the plate and see the ball come off the bat. This enables you to get
a good jump. Anticipation is important, too. Try to determine the
direction the batter will likely hit the ball. For example, if you
notice the batter swinging late, you can shade to the right or left.
If it's a weak hitter, you may want to play in a little bit. Knowing
the abilities and tendencies of the opposing batters as well as your
pitcher's strengths and weaknesses can be very helpful.

Drill

This is a simple drill that concentrates solely on charging the ball
with good balance while centering the ball on the belly button. The

player and coach stand in an open area, perhaps center field. The coach maintains a distance of about 10 feet from the player. The player gets in the setup position (knees bent, feet shoulder-width apart, glove at knee height, back straight, head up). The coach gently rolls a ball on the ground to the left or right. The player charges the ball (using the technique discussed earlier) and extends the glove so that the ball and glove are in the center of the player's body (at the belly button). Although the ball will have stopped by the time the player gets to it, the idea is to charge while under control, take shorter steps as the player gets closer to the ball, and center the ball on the player's body while getting the glove down and out in front. The coach again moves 10 feet away and repeats the drill.

While it is important to learn the proper technique, you never want to get your mind cluttered with so many things that you become like a robot. It is important to stay loose and relaxed. But how? By practicing the fundamentals so often that they become second nature— a part of you. Then you won't even have to think about them. This permits you to concentrate on the situations of the game (e.g., number of outs, location of the runners) so you'll know what to do or where to throw after catching the ball. You will be loose and relaxed—confident that you'll make the correct decision when the ball is hit.

That's why repetition is so important. If you consciously think about all the steps involved in catching a ground ball while in the process, your overall effectiveness will be reduced. Your fielding must be instinctive. The only way to do this is through practice. Your movements will be committed to memory and become automatic. You will become a more confident and better player.

22

INFIELDER'S FEAR OF THE BASEBALL

> *Acknowledging that you're frightened is no reflection upon your manliness, your strength, your talent, or your courage.*
> —Charley Lau, major-league player and batting instructor

When he spoke these words, famous major-league batting instructor Charley Lau was referring to the fear of being struck by a pitched ball. But fear is fear, regardless of how or when we experience it. It is a crippling emotion that can prevent us from performing to our potential. Therefore, we have nothing to fear but fear itself. In terms of fielding a ground ball, fear robs us of our confidence and aggressiveness—two essential elements of consistently successful infield play. Fear causes our bodies to become tense and rigid; it causes our minds to lose concentration.

Matador or Infielder?

It is easy to recognize players who are fearful of ground balls hit in their direction. Here are a few characteristics of such a player:

- Doesn't charge the ball aggressively
- Doesn't get in front of the ball
- Turns the head, arms, and shoulders as the ball arrives
- Backhands the ball to the side of the body
- Closes the eyes
- Makes an "olé" swipe at the ball while bailing out to the side and raising the body

The Solution

Fear is a response to your desire to protect your body, which unfortunately can surpass your desire to catch the ball. In addition to preventing you from making the play, fear can cause injury. For example, if you turn your head and take your eyes off the ground ball, you lose control over the situation and give up the ability to react to a bad hop.

If fear can cause you to turn your head as you field the ball, it is reasonable to say that looking the ball into the glove is one of the remedies. Of course, other things must be done correctly before that. First, get in front of the ball with your glove fully extended out in front. Keep your head down. If you look the ball all the way into the glove, you will eliminate the possibility of turning your head or raising your body. No need to worry; your reflexes will move your glove in time to catch the ball if it is misdirected. If not, the ball may harmlessly bounce off your chest, arm, or shoulder. You'll be surprised by how quickly your reflexes come to your rescue. But you must use good footwork and maintain your balance while keeping your eyes on the ball.

Fear of making an error or a mistake is a related problem that similarly reduces a player's effectiveness. Let's say you boot an easy ground ball during a game. Right away your confidence level plummets. You're still the same capable player physically; however, your mind tells you otherwise. Your mind is now the problem. So, what do you do to correct this? First, relax your body, especially your arms and hands. Remember how loose and relaxed you feel when you're fielding grounders during practice sessions. You're sure of yourself and can't wait for the next ball to be hit in your direction. Now, visualize making every play smoothly and successfully. The way you perform is the result of how you envision yourself doing it. Constantly create an image in your mind of who you want to be: a confident, loose, and excellent fielder. Think about it and become that fielder. What you think about is what you will focus on and create more of. You must remain positive. The way you think is the way you act, so choose to be positive. If you doubt your ability to make the play cleanly, there's a good chance you won't. Be in control of your thoughts. Your chances of making the play will increase.

If you do commit an error or mistake, whether mental or physical, consider it a learning opportunity. Value it as a necessary step in your development as a player. Analyze what just occurred, then put the lesson in your memory bank. It will put you in a positive frame of mind. Negativity stops the flow of energy and makes your movements tentative. Remember, there are important lessons to learn from whatever occurs to you, but you must pay attention to them if you are to grow as a ballplayer.

Very simply, the basic solution to overcoming fear is learning the fundamentals of catching ground balls and consistently employing them in practice and games. It gives you the most confidence and offers the best protection for your body. The more you practice the fundamentals, the more this will become evident.

Younger Players

Players at the Tee Ball level can start fielding grounders with tennis balls for a comfortable first experience. Begin by tossing grounders to them on a hard surface (e.g., parking lot or driveway). They'll learn the proper technique. Then move them to a grassy or dirt surface where they'll encounter bad hops that occasionally hit them in the arms or chest. Let them become accustomed to that feeling and the way their hands react quickly to the bad hops. Next, use a hard ball and throw them grounders; then hit them grounders. This kind of practice and repetition gradually builds confidence and reduces fear. Ideally, the players will want every ball hit to them during the game. That is the sign that fear has disappeared and confidence has taken over.

23

BACKPEDALING TO CATCH FLY BALLS

Paul Blair could stand in center field and know when a ball was hit over his head. He would turn around and run, get to a spot, and then look up—and there would be the ball. He'd grab it easily.

—Earl Weaver

Note that Paul Blair, Baltimore's great defensive center fielder, would run to a spot and catch the fly ball. He didn't backpedal—he took off in full flight. Backpedaling, which unfortunately is an instinctive reaction for many young players, can definitely cause trouble.

Backpedaling means running backward to reach a fly ball hit over your head. Instead of turning your body and running, you take steps backward while facing the infield. What is wrong with this? Plenty! First, you can't run as fast backward as you can forward. You can easily lose your balance or trip because running backward is awkward—especially when done at full speed. You can also lose

Backpedaling (as shown) to catch a fly ball is OK if the ball is hit only a few feet behind you. It is a mistake to attempt this when balls are hit several feet behind you.

156

sight of the ball as your head moves up and down with each step. And if you need to leap in the air to make the catch, you can't jump as high while running backward as you can forward.

Speed Is the Answer

Let's think again about the objectives: get to the ball as quickly as possible while maintaining your balance, keep the ball in your sight, be ready to jump if necessary, and move your body into the best position to make a throw after the catch. So, considering all this, what is the best way to run for a fly ball hit over your head? It all starts with the outfielder's proper setup position. Use a narrow stance with the weight on the balls of your feet and knees flexed. Keep your body more upright than an infielder's. Unlike the infielder, an outfielder is more likely

In the outfield, set up in an athletic position, hands in front and head up watching the pitcher and batter.

to run long distances or make a dash to reach the ball. Keep your glove and bare hand out in front of your body at knee height. Walk into this ready position as the pitcher delivers the ball. This gives you the flexibility and looseness to react and move quickly in any direction.

Rather than backpedaling toward a ball over your head, turn your body in the direction of the ball using a drop step (see Mistake 24, "Taking the First

When a ball is hit far over your head, the first move in catching it is to take a drop step, that is, a step 45 degrees to the rear (top). Then make a crossover step (bottom) and run to the spot you've judged the ball will land. You may glance up while running after two or three steps to confirm your judgment.

Step In," for an explanation) and run back to the ball with your body turned sideways—not facing the ball. This, by itself, prevents you from backpedaling. Run at top speed. Ideally, you want to arrive early enough to get a few feet behind the ball so you can take a couple of steps toward the ball as it comes down. This generates momentum for your throwing motion, increasing your velocity and improving accuracy.

Never float over to the ball and time the catch in full stride. This may look stylish but it won't help when you need to throw out a runner trying to advance another base. Make a commitment to catch every ball as if you need to make a strong throw to the infield—even if you don't. You will be forming a good habit. Never run with your glove extended; this only slows you down. Instead, run as if you don't have a glove on your hand. You will get there faster. If it's a lazy fly ball and time permits, take a rounded path to the ball. In other words, rather than going directly to the ball, encircle it by taking a banana-shaped route that allows you to approach the ball from back to front. This puts you into the best position to catch and throw. Outfielders who execute these fundamentals are a pleasure to watch.

Drill

Here is an easy drill designed to eliminate backpedaling. It doesn't require a ball—just a player and coach. The player stands 20 feet from the coach and moves into the ready position. The coach raises either the left or right hand, indicating to which side the ball is hit. In response, the player turns to the correct side and sprints back with the body sideways to the coach while looking up. The player stops sprinting after 10 yards and returns to the original position. The coach repeats the drill. The coach may choose to expand the drill by throwing a ball to either side of the player. Throwing the ball is more controllable than hitting it.

"THE CATCH"

Perhaps the most famous catch by an outfielder was made by center fielder Willie Mays of the New York Giants in the 1954 World Series. In fact, it is referred to as "The Catch." Vic Wertz of the Cleveland Indians hit a long fly ball well over Willie's head, about 460 feet into the deepest part of the Polo Grounds. Mays turned and ran as fast as he could in the direction he thought the ball would land. He kept the ball in his sight by looking over his shoulder while maintaining his balance and control. He extended his arms and caught the ball with two hands. Falling to his knees, he quickly spun up and made an accurate throw back to the infield. Willie made everything look easy. That's because he made the effort to do it the right way.

24

TAKING THE FIRST STEP IN

> *You observe a lot just by watching.*
>
> —Yogi Berra

Put Yogi in the ballpark *watching* baseball's outfield play and it's certain that he will *observe* that the way to get ahead is by taking the first step back. As Yogi might say, "You get ahead a lot by first not going forward."

In outfield play your first step can be crucial. An initial step in the wrong direction requires a counterstep that only delays your movement toward the ball. It may be only a split-second delay, but it could prevent you from catching the ball and completing the play in time.

Young players react in a variety of ways to a ball hit in the air. Many instinctively step forward at the crack of the bat, regardless of whether the ball is hit in front of them, behind them, or right at them. It takes practice to read the trajectory and speed of a ball off the bat and determine how far the ball will travel. But it is a necessary talent to acquire if you are going to consistently make the correct first step.

Fancy Footwork

As soon as you gauge the trajectory of the ball and realize that it is hit over your head, use the drop-back step. For instance, if you see the ball coming to your right side, just move your right foot back slightly and angle it to the right. Then cross your left foot over your right. This gets you sideways to the ball—where you should remain the full length of your run. In this position you can look over your shoulder easily while running back at full speed. The quicker you can get into this position the better. If the ball is hit directly over your head, drop step toward the side you feel most comfortable with. The drop-back step is not difficult; it just takes practice so that it becomes a natural reaction.

The drop step can be to the glove side or the throwing-arm side, but it is a mistake to lose sight of the ball (see player on left). During the drop step (with your eyes still on the ball) you quickly judge how far the ball will travel and where it will come down. After the drop step you turn and run. As you run to the spot where it will come down, look up to relocate the ball.

The Ball Is Coming Right at Me!

A ball hit directly at you sounds like an easy play, but it can cause some players to freeze and panic, especially if it is a line drive. Maybe that is because it rarely happens. How should you react to a ball that initially appears to be hit directly at you? First, don't take a step; remain still and closely focus on the flight of the ball. Assume that it will actually stay the course unless you can determine otherwise. Looks can be deceiving, meaning that fly balls or line drives can change direction. So always be suspicious of balls that look like they are easy catches. Line drives, for example, sometimes react like knuckleballs; that is, they're apt to move at the last moment—up, down, or sideways. High fly balls can be blown off course by windy conditions. Perhaps the best policy is to expect the unexpected. Maintain your balance (from your proper setup position) in case you need to react quickly to a change in direction. And if the ball happens to stay on its course, your balanced position lets you catch it easily.

163

Drill

Only a coach and player are needed for this drill. The player assumes the outfielder's setup position, about 10 feet in front of the coach; he points to the player's right or left side. The player then makes a drop step using the correct foot, properly angled. The player then crosses over with the other foot, positions the body sideways, and runs a few steps back. The coach repeats the drill. A thrown fly ball can be added to the drill.

Get the glove up early when you settle under fly balls. Keep the elbow of the glove arm under the glove whenever possible.

Fielding fly balls hit by a coach off a fungo bat is good practice, but it doesn't match the benefits from catching balls hit "live" off a pitched ball. "Live" hits often sink, slice, hook, rise, and knuckle. You are not likely to see any of these from a fungo bat. Imagine the number of "live" hits during a common batting practice session—hundreds! It's a great training opportunity. If you take your position in the outfield, you're sure to have plenty of balls hit in your general direction. Get in the ready position before each pitch and try to gauge the trajectory and velocity of each fly ball. See the ball early and follow it intently. React to each one correctly: drop step for balls over your head; stay put for balls hit right at you. A ball hit to left field by a left-handed batter usually slices toward the left-field foul line. A ball pulled to right field by a left-handed batter usually hooks toward the right-field line. You will find that this is an excellent way to simulate a real game situation and to become accustomed to the way balls truly react off the bat.

25

CATCHING THE BALL ABOVE THE HEAD

Catch the ball belt-high or chest-high so that you keep your eyes on the ball.

—Ken Griffey, Sr.

Raising your glove above your head can make even a routine fly ball more difficult to catch than necessary. In fact, some young players put the glove above their heads while they are running for the fly ball, which slows them down and makes tracking the ball a real adventure. It is hard to explain why players do this, but it should be corrected for a variety of reasons. First of all, the glove and your arms can block your vision of the ball's flight. You lose a sense of where your glove is in relation to the incoming ball—you just hope the glove will connect with the ball. And even if you do catch the ball, it takes longer to bring it down and get into the throwing motion. Also, your margin for error is slim. That is, if the ball travels farther than expected or the wind carries it beyond your reach, you are in an awkward and unbalanced position from which to react. Your body is too upright, your knees are too stiff, and your weight is probably back on your heels. In short, your body is not in a flexible, ready position.

Bring It Down

Remember your objective: to catch the ball securely and release it quickly and accurately. To accomplish this, you need to keep the ball in full sight—from the second it leaves the bat, all the way into the glove. For fly balls hit far over your head, you have no choice but to extend your glove as high and far as you can to reach it. That's fine, but be sure to run to the ball with your glove down at your side, and raise it only when you get close to the ball. For fly balls that you can reach comfortably and in time to get behind, follow these steps:

When camped under a "can of corn" (lazy fly ball), you have plenty of time to move your glove-side leg slightly forward in preparation for the quick return of the ball to the infield.

1. Center the incoming ball in the middle of your chest.
2. Turn your body slightly toward your throwing side, with the shoulder of your glove-hand side facing the direction you'll be throwing.
3. Step toward the ball.
4. Extend your arms forward slightly from your body, between your chin and chest, so you'll be able to see the ball over your glove.
5. Catch the ball with two hands.

Don't catch the ball over your glove-hand shoulder. It prevents you from focusing on the ball's path, and it is not a good position from which to adjust to balls that change direction. Never assume

When charging ground balls in the outfield, take the ball in front of the glove-side leg and foot.

that a fly ball will stay its course. Wind can alter its direction. Plus, batted balls have a tendency to hook, slice, and sink.

Drill

Here is a simple drill that requires only a player and coach, or two players. The player stands 20 feet from the coach and assumes the setup position. The coach throws a high fly ball directly to the player, giving the player plenty of time to step into it with the body turned slightly to the throwing side and catch it with the glove between chin and chest level. The coach later throws fly balls over the player's head, requiring the player to retreat and get behind the ball before making the same play.

Weather can play tricks on an outfielder. Although you can't control Mother Nature, it helps to be a constant observer of the weather and field conditions. Let's use wind as an example. Before the game and during warm-ups, check the wind conditions on the field. Look at the flags. If there are no flags, look at the trees. How strong is the wind? What direction is it blowing? Is it swirling? Gusting? If it's blowing toward the outfield, fly balls will naturally carry farther than normal. You may consider playing deeper in this situation. A strong wind can carry a fly ball far off course, so be ready for it. Keep track of the conditions throughout the game and remind your teammates.

Also, is the field dry or wet? Wet grass will slow down ground balls, whereas the opposite is true when the ground is dry and hard. Is the grass high or short? Similarly, ground balls roll slower in high grass than short grass. Where is the sun? Is it shining directly in your eyes as you look toward home plate? If so, you will need to use your glove as a shield to block the sun. But like everything else, this takes practice.

Index